Reference Assessment
and Evaluation

Reference Assessment and Evaluation has been co-published simultaneously as *Public Services Quarterly*, Volume 2, Numbers 2/3 2006.

Reference Assessment and Evaluation

Tom Diamond
Mark Sanders
Editors

Reference Assessment and Evaluation has been co-published simultaneously as *Public Services Quarterly*, Volume 2, Numbers 2/3 2006.

Routledge
Taylor & Francis Group
NEW YORK AND LONDON

First published by
The Haworth Press, Inc.
10 Alice Street
Binghamton, N Y 13904-1580

This edition published 2011 by Routledge

Routledge
Taylor & Francis Group
711 Third Avenue
New York, NY 10017

Routledge
Taylor & Francis Group
2 Park Square, Milton Park
Abingdon, Oxon OX14 4RN

Reference Assessment and Evaluation has been co-published simultaneously as *Public Services Quarterly*, Volume 2, Numbers 2/3 2006.

The development, preparation, and publication of this work has been undertaken with great care. However, the publisher, employees, editors, and agents of The Haworth Press and all imprints of The Haworth Press, Inc., including The Haworth Medical Press® and Pharmaceutical Products Press®, are not responsible for any errors contained herein or for consequences that may ensue from use of materials or information contained in this work. With regard to case studies, identities and circumstances of individuals discussed herein have been changed to protect confidentiality. Any resemblance to actual persons, living or dead, is entirely coincidental.

The Haworth Press is committed to the dissemination of ideas and information according to the highest standards of intellectual freedom and the free exchange of ideas. Statements made and opinions expressed in this publication do not necessarily reflect the views of the Publisher, Directors, management, or staff of The Haworth Press, Inc., or an endorsement by them.

Cover design by Kerry E. Mack.

Library of Congress Cataloging-in-Publication Data

Reference assessment and evaluation / Tom Diamond, Mark Sanders, editors.
    p. cm.
"Co-published simultaneously as Public services quarterly, volume 2, numbers 2/3, 2006."
Includes bibliographical references and index.
ISBN-13: 978-0-7890-3193-8 (alk. paper)
ISBN-10: 0-7890-3193-0 (alk. paper)
ISBN-13: 978-0-7890-3194-5 (pbk. : alk. paper)
ISBN-10: 0-7890-3194-9 (pbk. : alk. paper)
    1. Academic libraries–Reference services–United States–Evaluation. I. Diamond, Tom. II. Sanders, Mark, 1974- III. Public services quarterly.

Z711.R44325 2006
025.5'20973–dc22
                                                                        2006001667

Reference Assessment and Evaluation

CONTENTS

ABOUT THE EDITORS

Tom Diamond is the Head of Reference Services at Louisiana State University Libraries in Baton Rouge. He is a member of the American Library Association's Library Administration and Management Association (LAMA) division; within LAMA, he serves in the Measurement, Assessment and Evaluation Section and Public Relations Marketing Section. He is also a member of the Louisiana Library Association. Mr. Diamond is the author of the book, *The Economic and Political Aspect of the Tobacco Industry: An Annotated Bibliography and Statistical Review, 1990-2004* and the Association of Research Libraries Spec Kit (280) (June 2004), *Library User Surveys*. He has contributed articles to *RQ*, the *LLA Bulletin*, and *Louisiana Libraries*; he has co-contributed to *College & Research Libraries*.

Mark Sanders is the Student Outreach Reference Librarian at East Carolina University in Greenville, NC. He holds a BA in Foreign Languages from the University of North Carolina–Asheville, an MA in Spanish Literature from Penn State University, and an MLS from the University of North Carolina–Chapel Hill. He is active on the ACRL Marketing Academic and Research Libraries Committee and with the Reference and Adult Services Section (RASS) of the North Carolina Library Association.

Introduction

Many exciting developments and changes in academic library reference service have taken place over the past several years. New and innovative ideas, together with the constant evolution of technology, continue to alter the ways in which academic librarians meet the information needs of students, faculty, and researchers. Delivering consistent, high quality reference service is more important than ever with the increased competition many college and research libraries face from the rise of their patrons' exclusive reliance on Google and other Internet search engines. Consequently, the evaluation and assessment of service is one of the most important issues facing reference departments. This is especially true with respect to the increased pressure on administrations to meet fiscal goals, produce new research throughout all departments, and attract the most talented students and faculty to the academy. This work presents a number of methods, models, and case studies devoted to the evaluation and assessment of reference service in academic libraries.

We begin the volume with two case studies describing the efforts of librarians to develop, assess, and improve instruction in reference resources. At the University of Colorado at Boulder, the library implemented a drop-in research consultation program for undergraduates enrolled in the introductory writing course. Contributors from Colorado State University discuss their experiences coordinating an annual professional development program for specialized instruction targeted at faculty and staff members. Both of these initiatives subsequently administered assessment surveys to determine effectiveness and patron satisfaction.

[Haworth co-indexing entry note]: "Introduction." Diamond, Tom, and Mark Sanders. Co-published simultaneously in *Public Services Quarterly* (The Haworth Information Press, an imprint of The Haworth Press, Inc.) Vol. 2, No. 2/3, 2006, pp. 1-2; and: *Reference Assessment and Evaluation* (ed: Tom Diamond, and Mark Sanders) The Haworth Information Press, an imprint of The Haworth Press, Inc., 2006, pp. 1-2. Single or multiple copies of this article are available for a fee from The Haworth Document Delivery Service [1-800-HAWORTH, 9:00 a.m. - 5:00 p.m. (EST). E-mail address: docdelivery@haworthpress.com].

The work also includes a number of articles which examine the dynamics of reference desk interactions. Contributors from Augustana College Library and St. Ambrose University Library, separated by the Mississippi River, embarked upon an innovative peer observation exchange to achieve similar, but nevertheless different, assessment goals. In California, the San José State University Library merged its government publications desk with the reference services desk, which ultimately became merged with the public library's reference desk when the university and city embarked upon a unique collaboration of academic and public libraries. At Valparaiso University's main library, contributors discuss steps taken to assure that student assistants are properly prepared for the questions they will face when staffing the reference desk.

The future of reference chat service evaluation and assessment is represented in this volume as well. Contributors from the University of South Alabama's Baugh Biomedical Library discuss both the traditional reference and the digital reference evaluation methods used after one year of offering a chat service to patrons. At the University of Texas at Arlington's library, an article evaluates chat service from the point of view of the staff.

Finally, several articles discuss the results of statistical approaches to reference service evaluation and assessment. Contributors from the University of North Texas Libraries analyze sixteen years of reference statistics to determine relationships between technology and questions posed at the reference desk. At the University of Tennessee at Chattanooga, statistical models are used to determine library use and appropriate levels of staffing at the reference desk.

We hope that you enjoy and benefit from this publication. We encourage readers to consider the ways in which they can modify and use some of the models, methods, and ideas presented in the following pages at their own institutions.

Tom Diamond
Mark Sanders

Evaluating the Drop-In Center:
A Service for Undergraduates

Becky Imamoto

SUMMARY. The Reference Department at the University of Colorado at Boulder provides a research consultation service to undergraduates enrolled in the mandatory introductory writing course. The Research Center is staffed by graduate students trained in providing reference assistance. Librarians in the Reference Department administered a patron satisfaction survey to 415 students to evaluate the effectiveness of the Research Center. The survey addressed patron response to the research tutors, services offered, and overall satisfaction. Responses are overwhelmingly positive. Students used the Research Center most often on Mondays and between weeks 7 and 13 of the semester. *[Article copies available for a fee from The Haworth Document Delivery Service: 1-800-HAWORTH. E-mail address: <docdelivery@haworthpress.com> Website: <http://www.HaworthPress.com> © 2006 by The Haworth Press, Inc. All rights reserved.]*

KEYWORDS. Reference services, evaluation, bibliographic instruction, information literacy, college and university students, research consultation

Becky Imamoto is formerly the Undergraduate Services Librarian, University of Colorado, Boulder, CO (E-mail: imamoto@csus.edu). She is currently attending California State University, Sacramento.

[Haworth co-indexing entry note]: "Evaluating the Drop-In Center: A Service for Undergraduates." Imamoto, Becky. Co-published simultaneously in *Public Services Quarterly* (The Haworth Information Press, an imprint of The Haworth Press, Inc.) Vol. 2, No. 2/3, 2006, pp. 3-18; and: *Reference Assessment and Evaluation* (ed: Tom Diamond, and Mark Sanders) The Haworth Information Press, an imprint of The Haworth Press, Inc., 2006, pp. 3-18. Single or multiple copies of this article are available for a fee from The Haworth Document Delivery Service [1-800-HAWORTH, 9:00 a.m. - 5:00 p.m. (EST). E-mail address: docdelivery@haworthpress.com].

doi:10.1300/J295v02n02_02

INTRODUCTION

In 2000, the Reference Department at the University of Colorado at Boulder Libraries entered into a partnership with the Program for Writing and Rhetoric (PWR). PWR is a unit within the College of Arts and Sciences and is responsible for campus-wide instruction in expository writing. PWR's mission is to train "students to think critically about the texts they read and the writing they produce and to enable them to shape and express ideas with clarity and grace in any context" (2003, p. 1). The objective of the collaboration is to integrate information literacy concepts into the PWR's first-year writing course. The stated outcome is to teach students information literacy skills so that they can be successful in their college career. WRTG 1150 is a mandatory, introductory writing course for all College of Arts and Sciences students. Generally, students take WRTG 1150 as freshmen, and over 2,050 enrolled in the class during 2003-2004. The information literacy component of this partnership consisted of four segments:

1. WRTG 1150 students complete an online tutorial (comprised of six modules) designed to teach basic library research. Each module includes a quiz graded by the library.
2. All WRTG 1150 classes come to the library for a one-time course-integrated library seminar that expands on material taught in the online tutorial.
3. The library hosts a website at http://ucblibraries.colorado.edu/pwr/themes/themes.htm, which functions as a theme-based course reader of full-text, online articles for WRTG 1150 students (Knievel, 2003). Currently, there are 11 themes ranging from such topics as the environment, intellectual property, and scientific literacy.
4. The library operates a drop-in Research Center exclusively available for WRTG 1150 students.

During the 2003-2004 academic year, the Reference Department decided to review the fourth segment, the Research Center. The Undergraduate Services Librarian and the Humanities Reference Librarian, who coordinate partnership activities, agreed that an evaluation survey best served the purpose for discerning the users' expectations of the Research Center.

DESCRIPTION OF THE RESEARCH CENTER

The drop-in Research Center complements both the online tutorial and the library seminar. It is a further opportunity for the students to gain the information literacy skills of locating, evaluating, and using information. The Research Center offers one-on-one help accessing the course reader, completing the library tutorial, and finding resources for the students' research projects. This service is a type of research consultation, but it differs in three very important ways from the traditional one-on-one reference appointment: (1) it is a very informal environment with no appointment needed; (2) it is staffed by graduate students; and (3) it is open only to WRTG 1150 students, mainly freshmen, who are usually writing their first academic paper in college.

The Research Center is located in a large multi-purpose lab within the library. The Reference Department teaches library seminars in this lab from 8 a.m. to 3 p.m. At 3 p.m., the lab is turned over to the Research Center and the University Writing Center. This is an ideal situation since the two groups offer complementary services; students can receive both writing and research help in one location. The Research Center is open eight hours a week, Monday-Thursday from 3-5 p.m.

STAFFING-RESEARCH ASSISTANTS

Early on in the collaboration process, both departments realized this library instruction program would require a great deal of extra work that could not be absorbed by the librarians. Therefore, an agreement exists between the two partners that the University Libraries pays for one research assistant while PWR funds two, for a total of 50 hours per week among the three staff. The Reference Department supervises the research assistants. The research assistants play an integral part in running the day-to-day WRTG 1150 information literacy program. Their duties include assisting reference librarians with teaching a large portion of the library seminars (about half of them in the 2003-2004 school year), grading the six tutorial quizzes per student (which amounts to over 12,000 quizzes a year), staffing the Research Center, updating the reading themes, and performing other administrative tasks.

Research assistants come from PWR and the English department. They are hired based on their knowledge of the library and library research, and they must have teaching experience. Richard Bopp (1995) notes that since nonprofessionals (such as research assistants) "generally have not completed a full-formal educational program in reference service, a carefully designed training program for them is necessary if they are to provide accurate and effective service" (p. 23). Therefore, the research assistants go through a few weeks of vigorous training during the beginning of the school year. This training consists of:

1. Taking the tutorial
2. Reading through the quiz rubrics
3. Observing library seminars
4. Understanding the WRTG 1150 library seminar lesson plan
5. Sitting with librarians at the reference desk
6. Learning to use the most popular article databases
7. Working on sample Research Center questions

The last two training segments are the most important in terms of the research assistants' ability to help students in the Research Center. Generally, students come to the Research Center because they need help finding articles for their research paper. It is essential that the research assistants know which databases to suggest and also how to use them properly. It is emphasized during training that if the research assistants do not feel capable of answering a question, they should refer students to the subject librarians. All subject librarians are available for research consultations for in-depth research concerns.

RESEARCH CENTER EVALUATION

While feedback from PWR instructors, students, and librarians provides information about the library seminar, there is no formal evaluation of the Research Center. Are its services being used? If so, do students feel the services are helpful? What improvements can be made? Coleman, Hambric, and Fos (1997) state, "Customer feedback is essential for determining what elements constitute quality service in a reference department" (p. 25). Therefore, we decided to answer these questions with usage statistics and a user satisfaction survey.

LITERATURE REVIEW

The current literature on evaluation of reference service is quite extensive. There are many different models for carrying out reference evaluations that can be divided into four distinct approaches.

The first approach prefers to gather information by completing unobtrusive studies of interactions between reference librarians and patrons. Peter Hernon and Charles McClure (1986) completed the most famous study of this type. Hernon and McClure found that reference librarians answering a predetermined set of factual questions respond correctly only 55% of the time. Their results continue to be debated among librarians 20 years later. John Richardson, Jr. (2002) argued that Hernon and McClure's study used unsuitably small samples and that the study should include questions that required more than a yes/no response. He expanded the study to twelve public libraries and used a panel of reference experts to judge how well reference librarians performed. The experts "determined that librarians recommend an accurate source or an accurate strategy in response to a user's query" in 90% of the cases (p. 42). Elaina Norlin (2000) expanded on the unobtrusive model to include qualitative techniques such as satisfaction surveys and focus groups in her evaluation of reference desks at the University of Arizona. Norlin reasoned that a three-step approach created a complete evaluation because it included behavior traits with the unobtrusive questionnaire.

The second approach believes that there are other factors involved in customer satisfaction than just receiving the right answers. Joan Durrance (1989) is well known in the field for concentrating on the interpersonal communication process between the librarian and the patron. She looks at "the willingness of the inquirer to return to the staff member at a later time" (p. 32). Her research (1995) found that reference transactions are most successful when librarians are interested in the question, have good listening skills, ask open questions, and determine the need behind the question.

The third approach is the complex model used in the Wisconsin-Ohio Reference Evaluation Program. Murfin and Gugelchuk (1987) studied over 15 academic libraries (plus many public libraries) to collect data on the effectiveness of reference desk transactions by having both librarians and patrons fill out a computer-scanable form that analyzed 35 variables. Murfin and Bunge (1988) said this enabled "libraries to gather data on perceptions of question-answering success from both the librarian and the patron" (p. 11). This project concluded that multiple methods of evaluation should be used to effectively determine the success of reference services.

The fourth approach is a smaller sect that specializes in using qualitative research to decide, "what is meant by the term 'quality' as it applies to reference service" (p. 546). Jennifer Mendelsohn (1997) interviewed two librarians, a faculty member, and a graduate student and found that knowledge and willingness from the librarian are significant elements in determining a successful reference encounter.

After reviewing all the literature, we agreed with Murfin (1995) who said, "User input should be an essential dimension of evaluation of reference service" (p. 231). Taking this into account, along with the size and nature of the service and the desire for quantitative data, we decided to use a simple three-to-five question patron satisfaction survey.

METHODOLOGY

There are three objectives to this study: (1) discover how many students used the Research Center; (2) get a better understanding of the research needs of the student users; and (3) find out how the student users felt about the service provided. The author thought it best to keep the survey simple and concise in an attempt to attract the greatest number of respondents.

During the 2003-2004 school year, the Reference Department administered the survey. The Research Center opened and conducted business during the 3rd-16th week of each semester for eight hours a week. The Reference Department publicized the Research Center on the library tutorial web pages, at the library seminar, and relied on the PWR instructors to remind their students of its existence throughout the semester.

The research assistants took charge of gathering the usage statistics. After helping a student, they would record the date, the purpose of the visit, additional notes (if any), and then initial the form.

After completion of service, the research assistant would give an evaluation form to each student user. In the fall semester of 2003, this consisted of three simple questions:

1. Was the research tutor helpful?
2. What is the most useful element of the Research Center?
3. How would you improve the Research Center?

After examining the collected forms in December 2003, we realized a need for additional information. From the students' comments, we learned that they wanted the Research Center to have longer hours. We agreed with the students, but remained unsure which new hours would be preferred. Therefore, we added a fourth question to the questionnaire for the next semester:

4. If the Research Center opened two more hours a day, what hours would be the most useful to you? (Four options followed)

Finally, we considered the need to ask a general question about the student's experience at the Research Center. This turned into a fifth question:

5. Rate your overall experience with the Research Center on a scale of 1 to 5 (1 being the lowest).

The student dropped the completed form into a slotted box located in the Research Center. At the end of each month, the Undergraduate Services Librarian collected the forms and entered the information into a spreadsheet.

RESULTS AND ANALYSIS

Attendance

Four hundred and fifteen students used the Research Center during the 2003-2004 school year. This represented approximately 20% of the 2,050 enrolled in WRTG 1150.

As expected, student attendance reached its peak during the late middle of the semester (see Figure 1). These students came to the Research Center at their greatest time of need–when they started to work on their research paper/project (usually due near the end of the semester). In both semesters, the increase in student users started in week 7 and stayed strong until week 13. (Note: the drop in attendance during spring semester week 11 is due to the Library being closed during Spring Break.)

This data also proved that in the early weeks (3 through 6), few students used the Research Center. During that time period, there were 10 days with no student visitors and 7 days with only one student visitor. Next year, the Research Center will open on a later date in the semester to avoid staffing an empty room.

Figure 2 illustrates a breakdown of student attendance by days of the week. The Research Center opened 109 days, during which a total of 415 students used it; this averages to 3.8 student users per day. Monday served as the most popular day of the week with an average of 4.6 students. Following Monday, the rest of the week tracked a natural pro-

FIGURE 1. Research Center Attendance by Semester and Combined

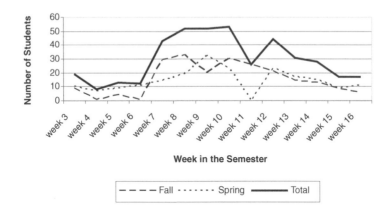

Week in the Semester

── ── Fall ······· Spring ━━━━ Total

FIGURE 2. Student Attendance by Week Day

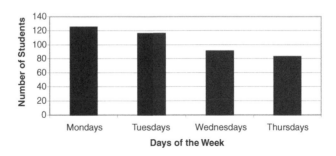

gression: Tuesday (4.1), Wednesday (3.2), and Thursday (3.1). It is possible that students who experienced difficulty finding research materials on the weekends realized that they needed assistance and decided to use the Research Center the following Monday. This data tells us that we should consider double staffing the Research Center on Mondays.

Purpose of Visit

The research assistants recorded each student's purpose in using the Research Center. As expected, the majority, 72%, requested help on their individual research needs; 16% wanted help completing the tutorial, and 12% experienced technical trouble (most likely accessing subscription databases from off-campus).

Satisfaction with Research Assistant

Ninety-five students out of 415 filled out the survey for a response rate of 23%. The summary of data shows an extremely high degree of satisfaction with the research assistant ("research tutor" on the survey). Ninety students (95%) agreed that the research tutor proved to be helpful. The following written comments typically described the research tutor:

1. "The tutor helped me find research for my paper."
2. "The Research Tutor showed me how I could find what I was looking for."
3. "She helped me locate two sources I needed desperately."
4. "The tutors are great because they generally want to help you and they don't get frustrated."

Five students chose not to answer this question, but no student described the research tutor as being unhelpful.

Initially, we wondered about the research assistants' ability to effectively help students with research. Did they receive enough training to help? A past study by Deese-Roberts and Keating (2000) proved that graduate student tutors "can enhance formal library instruction services by . . . help[ing] students gain fundamental library research skills" (p. 229). On the other hand, Murfin and Bunge (1988) completed a study on a service provided by paraprofessionals that "result[ed] in significantly lower patron success and satisfaction than that achieved by professional librarians" (p. 10). Beth Woodard's groundbreaking survey (1989) discovered that "nonprofessionals. . . can provide effective service to library patrons asking particular kinds of questions" (p. 464). These particular questions are ones with concrete answers where there is less room to answer incorrectly. While our survey did not address how accurately graduate students responded to student queries, it did tell us that the students overwhelmingly approved of them. We are therefore satisfied with our decision to use graduate students in lieu of librarians to staff the Research Center. Additional student comments about specific assistance that tutors provided include:

1. "The tutor helped me narrow down my topic into something manageable."
2. "He showed me how to make citations."
3. "She helped clarify if an article is scholarly."
4. "She showed me where things were located in the library."

Usefulness of Research Center

Students differed in identifying the most useful element of the Research Center (see Figure 3). Thirty-one percent felt the research assistant served as the most useful element. Twenty-one percent mentioned the availability of computers in the lab. (Other labs on campus can have a waiting period during the busy hours, but with 18 computers, the Research Center never had a problem accommodating students.) Seventeen students, a smaller number than expected, cited the free printing. The University of Colorado at Boulder had just changed to a pay-for-print model and our lab became one of the few remaining places on campus with a free printer. During the year, we noticed the popularity of the service by repeatedly having to ask students to leave who tried to slip into the lab while not participating in a library seminar. One thankful student wrote, "The ability to print for free was seriously helpful. It gives latitude to do research without worrying about printing cost." Fifteen percent of respondents noted the on-demand, drop-in aspect of the Research Center as the most important element. According to one,

FIGURE 3. Most Useful Element of Research Center

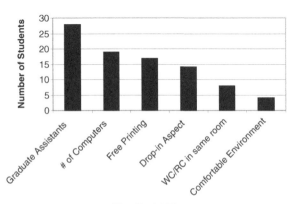

Most Useful Element

"One-on-one knowledgeable attention is great. Thanks for not making me make an appointment! I can't think of a better way to learn." This statement proved gratifying because it showed that the informal atmosphere made the Research Center an inviting and welcoming place. Nine percent noted the importance of having the Writing Center located in the same room. One student remarked, "I love that I can get help on my writing and then walk across the room to the Research Center for research help. Very convenient." Since this represented the original concept behind the shared space, we are pleased that students recognized the complementary nature of the two centers. Finally, a small group nominated the comfortable environment as the most important element. One wrote, "The chairs are nice and cozy."

A very satisfied student responded, "I wish I knew what this place was all about earlier; I would have been coming all semester." The variety of answers prove that the Research Center is useful to students in many different ways, including some that we would have considered–such as comfortable chairs. It seems that all the different elements added together create satisfied users: knowledgeable tutor + good facilities + accommodating room = quality service.

Areas for Improvement

Analysis of this question provided further proof of the success of the Research Center. Thirty-nine students felt the Research Center did not need to be changed or improved while 13 students skipped the question. We assume that a large portion of the thirteen who skipped this question did so because they did not think of anything needed to improve the Center. If this is a correct assumption, then over 50% of respondents saw no room for improvement–a good indication that the Research Center is providing a needed and beneficial service.

We did, however, receive a few valuable suggestions for improvement. These included 15 requests for additional hours, and so extended hours for the Research Center are under consideration. The half-dozen requests for more tutors on duty have led us to consider double-staffing the Research Center on Mondays (highest-use day) and during the busiest weeks of the semester. An additional six students asked for Microsoft Office to be loaded on the lab computers. This had been avoided in the past for fear of spreading computer viruses and to keep the lab from becoming a word processing lab instead of a research lab. However, the logic of offering word processing software cannot be denied, and with proper security restrictions in place we will offer this service next fall. In response to five students complaining about the difficulty in locating the Research Center, we created an online map highlighting the lab in the library. This map will be on every tutorial web page and linked from other appropriate websites. Four other students remarked on the lack of advertising for the Research Center. In response, we plan to post fliers about the Research Center in the PWR building. A couple of the requests did not fall under our control (e.g., more journal subscriptions), while others could not be feasibly implemented (e.g., play classical music and change location of the Research Center).

Without these student comments, we would be unaware of some problems that can easily be remedied. It is interesting to note that the students asked for more hours, additional tutors, and better publicity. These are the same areas for improvement that Rothstein wrote about in his 1989 article, and Kisby, Kilman, and Hinshaw mentioned in 1999. This might suggest areas of consistent weakness in library service.

Longer Hours at the Research Center

For fall semester 2004, we will be offering a new pilot Friday Research Center hour from 3-4 p.m. (see Figure 4). We are hoping that the additional hour on Friday will ensure that some students who might not have been able to use the Research Center in its 3-5 p.m. time slot will now have the opportunity to do so. We are also considering extending our 3-5 p.m. time to 3-6 p.m. Previously, we thought that students would not want to use the Research Center during the evening dinner hour so we closed at 5 p.m. Fifteen respondents (33%) selected the 5-7 p.m. time frame and this invalidated our assumption.

Research Center Experience

Responses from spring 2004 demonstrate how much students valued the Research Center (see Figure 5). We are pleased to note that the Research Center received zero low scores (1 or 2) and that 83% of the students gave a score of 4 or 5 for their overall experience in the Research Center (see Figure 5). Almost all who used the Research Center believed it to be helpful, informative, and useful. These findings are similar to what Kisby et al. (1999) discovered by surveying members of the Bibliographic Instruction Listserv (now ILI-L). Ten out of 12 libraries reported "levels of satisfaction such as very popular, wonderful, and positive" when asked about the success of their research consultation programs (p. 93).

FIGURE 4. Requested Research Center Hours

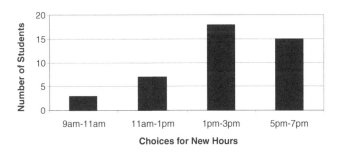

FIGURE 5. Rate Your Experience

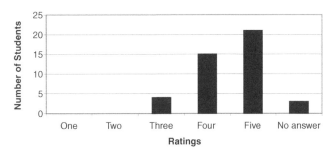

RESEARCH CENTER IMPACT ON REFERENCE SERVICE

While it is impossible to say whether all 415 students would have sought help at the reference desk if the Research Center did not exist, we can assume that a portion of them would have. When this author viewed statistics from the reference department, it showed that the number of transactions decreased steadily each semester by an average of 9% since we opened the Research Center. This decrease can be explained by a myriad of factors, one of which, most likely, is the availability of the Research Center. Even with the 9% decrease in transactions, the number of reference staff at the desk has not changed. The Reference Department currently staffs the reference desk with only one reference librarian or paraprofessional at a time and, therefore, could not decrease in number. In terms of instruction, the Research Center has become a welcome support for librarians. The average library seminar is 50 minutes, and sometimes that is not quite enough time to work individually with all students. Library instructors know that WRTG 1150 students have the opportunity to visit the Research Center for further assistance. Any sources or concepts that may have been covered too quickly in the seminar can be discussed again in a one-on-one setting. The Reference Department will continue to evaluate the Research Center once a year as a means to improve the quality of service provided.

IMPACT ON COLLABORATION WITH PWR

We have shared our data with the PWR faculty, and they are as pleased as the Reference Department with the results. Although there is always room for improvement, we can safely say that WRTG 1150 students appreciate the services provided by the Research Center. Hopefully, our data will ensure that PWR instructors continue to encourage their students to visit the Research Center. The results of the survey have only served to strengthen the ties between PWR and the Reference and Instructional Services Department.

AREAS FOR FURTHER STUDY

Due to the voluntary nature of the survey, only 23% of students completed a form, making this a lower sample than we would have liked. Next year, the research assistants will need to be more vigilant in handing out evaluation forms (sometimes they forgot, or were too busy with other students). We will also provide a designated quiet area for students to fill out their forms which we hope will elicit more responses.

We used a traditional user satisfaction survey, which does have its drawbacks. Coleman et al. (1997) stipulates "users will often report satisfaction even if the information received is not entirely useful because they appreciate personal assistance" (p. 29). Even though students are satisfied, are they getting the help they need? It would be interesting to next attempt an unobtrusive study to determine the graduate students' ability to assist in finding quality research for the students. Hernon and McClure (1986) define unobtrusive testing as "the process of asking reference questions (for which answers have been predetermined) of library staff members who are unaware that they are being evaluated" (p. 37). It would also be interesting to learn when and how often research assistants refer students to subject specialists.

This author would also like to revise the survey to record more information such as:

1. Are the students first time or repeat visitors?
2. Where or from whom did the students first find out about the Research Center?
3. What is the average length of time a graduate student spends with each student?

This information will provide more background information on the student users and further assist in the improvement of the Research Center services.

Finally, it would be interesting to discover to what extent the Research Center is lending itself to teaching information literacy objectives. We could accomplish this by asking questions such as:

1. Are students learning the research process or are they just getting the answers to their questions?
2. Are the PWR instructors seeing a marked improvement in the student users' research after visiting the Research Center?

CONCLUSION

The patron satisfaction survey of the Research Center provided the Reference and Instructional Services Department with valuable information. We discovered that (1) a significant portion of WRTG 1150 students visited the Center; (2) these student users considered the Research Center to be an extremely useful service; (3) they provided meaningful suggestions for improvement; and (4) graduate assistants, when trained properly, can provide quality service. Our findings agree with Kisby's et al. (1999) conclusion that research consultation "programs can be successful with any format, any amount of preparation time, and any audience" (p. 95). Overall, the Research Center is an integral element comprising the information literacy component of the partnership between the Reference Department and the Program for Writing and Rhetoric. We hope that our successful evaluation of the Research Center will serve as a model for other reference services at the University Libraries.

REFERENCES

Bopp, R. E., & Smith, L. C. (1995). *Reference and information services: An introduction.* Englewood, CO: Libraries Unlimited.

Bunge, C. (1990). Factors related to output measures for reference services in public libraries: Data from thirty-six libraries. *Public Libraries, 29*(1), 42-47.

Coleman, V., Hambric, L., & Fos, D. (1997). Tiered reference services: A survey. *The Reference Librarian, 59,* 25-35.

Deese-Roberts, S., & Keating, K. (2000). Integrating a library strategies peer tutoring program. *Research Strategies, 17*(2/3), 223-229.

Durrance, J. (1989). Reference success: Does the 55 percent rule tell the whole story? *Library Journal, 114,* 31-36.

Durrance, J. (1995). Factors that influence reference success: What makes questioners willing to return? *The Reference Librarian, 49/50,* 243-265.

Hernon, P., & McClure, C. (1986). Unobtrusive reference testing: The 55 percent rule. *Library Journal, 111*(7), 37-41.

Kisby, C., Kilman, M., & Hinshaw, C. (1999). Extended reference service in the electronic environment. *Information Technology and Libraries, 18*(2), 92-95.

Knievel, J. (2003). Library databases as writing-course anthologies: Implications of a new kind of online textbook. *Public Services Quarterly, 1*(4), 67-79.

Mendelsohn, J. (1997). Perspectives on quality of reference services in an academic library: A qualitative study. *RQ, 36*(4), 544-557.

Murfin, M. E. (1995). Evaluation of reference service by user report of success. *The Reference Librarian, 49-50,* 229-241.

Murfin, M. E., & Bunge, C. A. (1988). Paraprofessionals at the reference desk. *The Journal of Academic Librarianship, 14*(1), 10-14.

Murfin, M. E., & Gugelchuk, G. M. (1987). Development and testing of a reference transaction assessment instrument. *College & Research Libraries, 48*(4), 314-338.

Norlin, E. (2000). Reference evaluation: A three-step approach–surveys, unobtrusive observations, and focus groups. *College & Research Libraries, 61*(6), 546-553.

Program for Writing and Rhetoric. (n.d.). Retrieved January 12, 2005, from http:// www.colorado.edu/pwr/.

Richardson, Jr., J. V. (2002). Reference is better than we thought. *Library Journal, 127*(7), 41-42.

Rothstein, S. (1989). Point of need/maximum service: An experiment in library instruction. *The Reference Librarian, 25/26,* 253-284.

Woodward, B. (1989). The effectiveness of an information desk staffed by graduate students and nonprofessionals. *College & Research Libraries, 50*(4), 455-465.

Forward Progress One Step at a Time: Workshops, Assessment, and the Reference Connection

Catherine L. Cranston
Allison V. Level

SUMMARY. Library instruction about reference materials, databases, and quality web sites never goes out of fashion for students, faculty, or staff. An annual professional development program on the Colorado State University campus offers an opportunity to provide specialized library instruction to targeted faculty and staff members. For two consecutive years, the authors offered a workshop called "'Find it Fast': Research Tips for People in a Hurry." Using a standardized assessment tool, attendees were asked to rank their level of satisfaction with various aspects of the instruction session. By evaluating and incorporating this feedback, the authors modified and enhanced the workshop's format and content. Higher levels of user satisfaction are achieved in the second year, along with recommendations to continue and broaden the workshop. *[Article copies available for a fee from The Haworth Document Delivery Service: 1-800-HAWORTH. E-mail address: <docdelivery@haworthpress.com> Website: <http://www.HaworthPress.com> © 2006 by The Haworth Press, Inc. All rights reserved.]*

Catherine L. Cranston is Reference and Instruction Librarian (E-mail: Cranston@library.colostate.edu); and Allison V. Level is Agricultural Reference Librarian (E-mail: alevel@manta.colorado.edu), both at Colorado State University, 50 University Avenue, Fort Collins, CO 80523-1019.

[Haworth co-indexing entry note]: "Forward Progress One Step at a Time: Workshops, Assessment, and the Reference Connection." Cranston, Catherine L., and Allison V. Level. Co-published simultaneously in *Public Services Quarterly* (The Haworth Information Press, an imprint of The Haworth Press, Inc.) Vol. 2, No. 2/3, 2006, pp. 19-32; and: *Reference Assessment and Evaluation* (ed: Tom Diamond, and Mark Sanders) The Haworth Information Press, an imprint of The Haworth Press, Inc., 2006, pp. 19-32. Single or multiple copies of this article are available for a fee from The Haworth Document Delivery Service [1-800-HAWORTH, 9:00 a.m. - 5:00 p.m. (EST). E-mail address: docdelivery@haworthpress.com].

KEYWORDS. Assessment, instruction, reference, faculty workshops, academic libraries

INTRODCUTION

Everyone is on an information seeking journey of some kind. With the plethora of resources and Google searches returning hundreds of thousands of hits, getting information is not the problem. Obtaining the key and necessary information in a convenient format that quells the information need is the answer. The continual growth of reference books, online databases, government web sites, industry reports, technical overviews, and statistics mean that many researchers need help with the process of honing in on critical information. Librarians are there to provide this help. As Hinchcliffe and Woodard (2001) discuss, "When reference librarians approach a reference question with an instructional philosophy, not only do they provide the information that users need, they also capitalize on the opportunity to utilize the experience as a teaching moment" (p. 182). Librarians take advantage of these teachable moments whether at the reference desk, in the classroom, or in conversations with faculty or students. Elmborg (2002) defines a teachable moment as "one in which the student arrives at a position where he or she is open to teaching" (p. 461). The idea of teaching at every opportunity can and should be taken a step further. By expanding this mindset, librarians can think of assessment moments as the point when librarians are open to and encourage feedback.

The word "assessment" often brings up ideas of a capital letter "Assessment," with the requisite time commitment of a multi-faceted project. Instead of being burdened with the idea of a huge assessment project, thinking of assessment on a step-by-step basis can be beneficial to the entire instructional environment. Learning to recognize and capitalize on assessment moments benefits everyone involved in the information seeking process. Most authors make the connection of assessment to the student learning environment (Brown, 1997; Palomba & Banta, 1999). Beyond the college classroom, libraries are learning environments that reach a wider audience than students.

With this in mind, a pair of librarians at Colorado State University (CSU) Libraries started the journey to improved faculty satisfaction with library instruction. Using feedback from an evaluation form for a faculty workshop, a whole series of instruction sessions blossomed. One session grew into six which then transplanted momentum into more individual research consultations, follow-up encounters at the reference desk, and future plans for other faculty workshops, proving even small steps can yield great strides.

REFERENCE-INSTRUCTION CONNECTION

In the minds of some patrons, the need for a reference desk encounter has been preempted by Google or Yahoo! for ready reference questions (Janes, 2003). But more savvy researchers know that Google is not a substitute for the reference desk, just as online tutorials are not a substitute for all instruction programs. Reference and instruction have a symbiotic relationship. Saunders (2003) found that each student receiving bibliographic instruction increased reference traffic by two to seven questions, after an analysis of data collected over six years in 83 academic libraries belonging to the Association of Research Libraries (ARL). Saunders went on to say, "It appears as though instruction in bibliographic skills makes the student a more sophisticated library user, which in turn increases the student's demand for reference services" (p. 38). There may be other reasons for an increase in reference activities. Cardwell (2001) remarks that "excellent reference desk service goes beyond interaction between the librarian and user at the desk. The quality of service improves when faculty have confidence in librarians' abilities and expertise" (p. 257).

Not all libraries have an integrated reference and instruction model. Sometimes instruction librarians teach, but do not have reference desk responsibilities. As McCutcheon and Lambert (2001) demonstrate, "Often modes of communication between the two services are not formalized; the content of the well-conceived lecture delivered by a librarian to a class for a specific course assignment is unknown to the librarians staffing the reference desk" (p. 203). Organizational structures can benefit from the uniting of these two functions. For the library faculty at CSU, this connection is seen as mutually advantageous.

At CSU, the majority of public service librarians have responsibilities of reference, instruction, and collection development. The intertwining of these three areas creates a braided structure stronger than separate stand-alone threads. Each of these areas is not a discreet undertaking. Questions and research topics discussed at the reference desk provide a foothold into the classroom. This insight provides opportunities to develop assignments with faculty, promote the library's instruction program, and influences collection development decisions. In an article about information literacy in the reference environment, Rader (2000) highlights the need for these linkages, "In the digital information environment reference services and information skills instruction need to become integrated to offer library users and information seekers the most convenient and supportive learning environment" (p. 31). Reference and instruction should not be on parallel tracks. As Hinchliffe and Woodard (2001) succinctly put it, "To separate instruction from reference or reference from instruction is to do a disservice to users" (p. 182). The advantage of linking these information seeking skill sets means one part of work informs the others.

TAKING THE FIRST STEPS TOWARD ASSESSMENT

Trends in higher education assessment focus on a student-centered learning outcomes approach. Knight (2002) points out that measuring student-centered learning is difficult in a library setting for a variety of reasons, one being that librarians typically have only one or two meetings with the same group of students. Despite this difficulty with the process, articles about assessment of student learning abound in library journals. There is also no lack of information on the topic of instruction for a faculty audience. However, finding threads that tie these topics together (i.e., the assessment of faculty learning after a one-shot instruction workshop) is not a fruitful undertaking. Because it has not been widely researched, assessment of faculty learning is easy to overlook when planning instruction. An opportunity presented itself to fill this gap in the literature, as well as improve teaching methods for this audience.

In a recent editorial, Rockman (2002b) states, "Assessment strategies that are realistic, clear, coherent, communicated, manageable, sustainable, and integral to the educational mission of the institution have the greatest potential to yield meaningful results" (p. 181). This comprehensive view of assessment strategies is a good place to start when approaching an overall assessment plan. A realistic strategy in the case of a one-shot faculty workshop is to implement a simple evaluation instrument and use it to its full potential to improve the quality of future workshops. When faced with a tight schedule, a busy audience, and potentially only one meeting with the faculty member, the simpler the assessment form the better. Librarians and teaching faculty collaborate in many ways; building the collection, individual research, and setting up instruction for their students. Breivik and McDermand (2004) point out, "An essential ingredient in successfully integrating information competence into the curriculum is the quality of the relationships among the librarians and the classroom faculty" (p. 210).

Subject librarians have the opportunity to establish partnerships with faculty in the disciplines and therefore are able to develop a sense of how much faculty are tuned in to the new library tools and resources. If a comprehensive assessment of faculty learning is desired, it is better suited to this type of well-established faculty/librarian relationship. However, this does not mean that the chance to take advantage of an assessment moment when it presents itself should be overlooked. Assessment is an ongoing process, and it is not an end in itself but a vehicle for improvement (Agee & Gibson, 2004; Banta et al., 1996). Until an overall assessment of faculty learning is in place, small steps toward assessment should be taken.

WORKSHOP BACKGROUND AND PURPOSE

In January 2003 and 2004, a set of workshops called "'Find it Fast': Research Tips for People in a Hurry" was offered to CSU faculty and staff as part of the University's Professional Development Institute (PDI), sponsored by the Office of Instructional Services (OIS). The mission of OIS is to assist in enhancing CSU's programs in instruction, research, outreach, and service. As an integral part of these responsibilities, OIS has provided these PDI workshops for the past 25 years during which the Libraries has offered many sessions to faculty on a variety of specific topics. In her article about library assignment workshops for faculty, Mosley (1998) notes that participation in instruction sessions has a history of being erratic and it is sometimes difficult to attract busy faculty members to attend. This has also been the case at CSU with past workshops drawing from two to thirty participants. The low participation rate could be due to the fact that faculty look at information literacy training as remedial and perhaps only appropriate for students (Cunningham & Lanning, 2002).

The "Find it Fast" workshops were intended to provide a quick overview of the latest tools offered at the CSU Libraries which would make the work of a busy academic more efficient. Team-taught by library reference faculty, the original workshop was created based on a perceived interest by faculty and staff to learn about new services and databases offered by the library. It also provided an opportunity for people to tune up their technology and research skills. Keeping up with the changing technology used in library research is important to faculty for their own research, and for the pursuit of active literacy and lifelong learning (Purdue, 2003; Reeves et al., 2003).

Faculty, in particular, are engaged in their own research process and eager to learn new tools of the research trade (Bodi, 2002). As Hall (1999) observes, "If the faculty don't understand library research, how can they help their students learn to do it?" (p. 29). The faculty at CSU attended the "Find it Fast" workshops in high numbers. The ACRL *Guidelines for Instruction Programs in Academic Libraries* (2003, June) recommend that libraries make learning opportunities available in a variety of formats. Just like students, some faculty prefer to conduct research from their office, and perhaps interact with a subject librarian or the reference desk when they have a question, while other faculty also take advantage of face-to-face workshops that offer new research tips in a hands-on classroom setting (Cardwell, 2002).

FIRST YEAR WORKSHOP

In 2003, the "Find it Fast" workshop had a general outline which included pinpointing good starting points for research, finding reference books on a topic, and selecting the best databases for researching particular subjects. Specifically, the outline for the session included: finding reference books by using the catalog, an online tutorial called "Five Steps to Better Research," three database demonstrations including the new SFX (OpenURL) tool, web searching, and the new services, Citation Linker and MetaLib.

The 2003 class was advertised successfully, with the pre-registration enrollment filling the room and over thirty people on the waiting list. Although originally planned for two hours, it was decided the title "Find it Fast" suggested a shorter time frame, so the decision was made to compress the content into only one hour. All this was organized in an outline and timed with examples at the ready. There was time built in for the attendees to have hands on practice.

The librarians received a list of attendees prior to the session. Most of the audience had home departments in science and technology, so the expectation was that the group would be technologically savvy. This assumption turned out to be true. Despite being well rehearsed, and carefully mapped out, the librarians found themselves running out of time by the end of the hour, and squeezing in the last of their examples as time ran out. The carefully scripted session was somewhat flawed because planning did not allow enough time for the inevitable questions which savvy researchers pose. These were academic faculty and staff who were motivated to spend part of a day during their January break getting their research techniques up to speed. Such a motivated audience is going to ask substantial questions, and it would not have made sense to rigidly stick to the schedule if it meant turning off an interested library user by ignoring their questions.

At the end of the workshop, participants filled out the generic evaluation form. The instrument (see Appendix) used was a standard tool distributed by the coordinator of the OIS Professional Development Institute, and was therefore not specific for the library based workshop. The one-page form consisted of several Likert scale questions and space for comments. On a five-point scale that ranged from poor to excellent, participants were asked to rank:

- Overall session
- Content presented
- Presenter's delivery of content
- Presenter's knowledge of the topic
- Integration of graphics and/or visual aids

The attendees were then asked to rate their level of agreement with the following statements: This session met my professional/personal needs; I would be interested in attending a follow up session(s) on this topic; Future sessions on this topic should be from a perspective outside of CSU. There was a final set of questions that asked for general comments about the session and suggestions for future PDI topics.

When assessment is the goal, clearly it is "important to know how you are going to use the information before you design the instrument" (Williams, 2000, p. 323). Since the original workshop goals did not include assessment, the evaluation sheet was not modified from the original OIS version. Instead, it was expected that this evaluation sheet would be turned into the PDI coordinators for their review, however copies were kept for our files. Even if assessment had been given more thought prior to the session, it would have been impractical to ask faculty and staff to take a pre-/post-test, or to have them complete a more substantial evaluation sheet. That also would have taken too much time out of an already packed schedule.

FIRST YEAR FINDINGS

The comments from the session were mostly positive. The overwhelming suggestion for improvement was to allow more time for the session in the future. In fact, there were several people who requested future sessions with more hands-on time themselves. The Likert scale questions were positive, but the open-ended comments section provided the most useful information.

By using the same assessment tool from year to year, we were able to make an honest comparison between each year's successes based on the attendees' responses. The feedback that came through loud and clear from the first year's session was that there was too much content in too short a time frame. The compression of the two hour program into one hour was short sighted. The workshop result was only wholly satisfactory to those attendees who already had experience with most of the library's online tools. The rest of the audience, however, left feeling somewhat overwhelmed. Some comments included:

- Handouts good, would have helped if mentioned them in regard to each topic–things went fast and didn't always realize when there was a handout on a topic
- Please make it longer to allow for practice and questions
- Give these two presenters at least two hours next time, very concise and well delivered, tons of information–great
- Well prepared, fun, for 50 minutes = too much too fast, just too much to present in too little time, this covered a lot of material VERY QUICKLY, fast, nice overview and tips
- Some of it was very basic, but nice to learn about new library resources, way too much to deliver in a measly hour! But they did cover quite a lot, with good handouts and materials to refer to later, rushed

USE OF FINDINGS

It is important to take survey data and apply it in a tangible way when creating new programming efforts (McCord & Nofsinger, 2002). After reading the evaluations from the first PDI and looking at a waiting list of 30 people, the decision was made to offer a series of workshops on the same topics throughout the spring semester. Participants of the original workshop and everyone on the waiting list were contacted to let them know that additional sessions would be offered. In their article, Westbrook and Tucker (2001) pose some of the basic questions to begin with

"...What information needs do the faculty have?... What information do they want? What information skills do they have or want to gain? What information channels and formats most interest them? What information problems most concern them?" (p. 144). Unlike students who are at times required against their will to take a library class, the audience at the PDIs and follow-up sessions had self-selected. They did this during their winter break or busy spring semester, so they showed a strong motivation just by being there.

The initial PDI workshop spawned additional faculty and librarian contact. The librarians answered individual follow-up research questions, noticed some familiar faces at the reference desk, and generated more subject-based student classes brought in by the faculty. When the call for programs went out for the 2004 PDI sessions, the librarians decided to make modifications to the original workshop and offered the session again. In 2004, interest in the program was strong, and the class was filled for a second year.

SECOND YEAR WORKSHOP

The workshop plan for 2004 changed significantly. The first change was to schedule a full two-hour time slot for the presentation. After reviewing the outline, instruction topics were streamlined and, unlike the first year, there was a segment of the session devoted specifically to practice time and questions. With the two-hour format, follow-up sessions were unnecessary. The librarians were able to use a more relaxed pace while delivering the session content for a much improved teaching style. Another change for the second year was the inclusion of more extensive handouts that were color coded and compiled in a take-home folder. An expanded web page was used throughout the class, and also served as a way for the attendees to follow up independently after the session. The use of the web page emphasized the fact that library resources are not limited to a fixed place (Rettig, 2003). The combination of classroom lecture, extensive handouts, and the carefully crafted web page expands the librarian's teaching reach.

SECOND YEAR FINDINGS

The assessment tool used with these workshops remained unchanged from the first year to the second. The evaluations from the 2004 session reflected greater satisfaction with the workshop. Comments included:

- This was an extremely helpful session
- The first web searching class that has met my needs, I'm really looking forward to putting this to use
- Helpful presentation, great handouts, exceeded expectations, would have like more hands on woven into presentation–however, acknowledge time limitation, more time to practice while the new info is fresh would be nice. However, you did a great job squeezing a lot of info into two hrs
- Handouts are very helpful, knowledgeable and enthusiastic in sharing great library tools
- Not enough time! It was great! Should be a full day session! Great handouts and organization of session

The most obvious difference in the evaluations was that most people felt the two-hour time frame was the right length for the material covered. Only a couple of participants indicated that they wanted a longer session, one even suggesting an all day event. Resolving the problem of timing will never be perfect for everyone, but the change to the two-hour format seemed to make the rest of the minor problems with the previous year's delivery go away as well. Other than the comments about time frame, there were no substantive complaints about the second year workshop.

SUCCESS FACTORS

A workshop can be a foot in the door to developing relationships that lead to more cooperation and assessment opportunities. The impact of these PDI sessions on the attendees was felt for the remainder of the semester and beyond. It spurred many things to happen. Several faculty attendees were referred to their subject specialist librarians for follow-up with individual research projects or individualized instruction sessions for their classes. As Rockman (2002a) mentions, for assessment to be a success, partnerships between librarians and discipline-based classroom faculty are key. The popularity of the "Find it Fast" session, as evidenced by full classrooms plus an extensive waiting list, triggered the effort to continue to reach this audience.

By collaborating with the CSU's Computer Training and Support Services (CTSS), a series of subject-specialized offerings were developed for delivery outside of the library. The CTSS classes are typically software based instruction sessions led by Information Technology instructors, but the library was able to use their advertising and classroom space as a means of further reaching out to the faculty and staff on campus. The CTSS classes are just one example of instruction and outreach opportunities provided by the CSU Libraries. Neely et al. (2002) discuss in more detail examples of recent programs for distance learners, services to specific populations, and cooperative extension.

CONCLUSION

The way people seek and research information has dramatically changed. This is due in part to technological changes, but also because of conceptual changes, interdisciplinary studies, and new information seeking behaviors (Case, 2002). What started out as a one-time, one-hour workshop to address information seeking needs among faculty, continues to have impact. The "Find it Fast" workshops provided an opportunity for faculty outreach and set in motion an assessment moment. In the future, these moments will be linked and coordinated with the larger assessment plan for the instruction program. This coordination will involve looking internally and externally, as Lindauer (1998) concludes, "Assessing impact becomes a way of organizational thinking about how academic libraries are linked to the overall educational enterprise" (p. 561).

Further work for a third year of faculty PDI workshops has been postponed. The budget axe fell on the PDI programs and CSU has cancelled this program for 2005. However, the lessons learned from each of the workshops will continue to be incorporated in instruction. Continuing on this journey, some questions to consider include:

- What work needs to be done on assessing faculty learning?
- With constant technological change, what considerations need to be incorporated into outreach for faculty?
- How can librarians spread the concept of "assessment moments" across all encounters with instruction?

Now that the outlook of assessment has shifted from a thousand-mile journey to a series of manageable steps, assessment moments will be the lasting outcome of these workshops.

REFERENCES

Agee, A. S., & Gibson, C. (2004). Justify our love: Information literacy, student learning, and the role of assessment in higher education. In Gresham, K. (Ed.) *Information literacy and the technological transformation of higher education: Papers and documents of the ACRL Instruction Section Think Tank III* (p. 31-49). Ann Arbor: Pierian Press.

Association of College and Research Libraries (2003, June). *Guidelines for instruction programs in academic libraries.* Retrieved September 20, 2004, from the Association of College and Research Libraries website: http://www.ala.org/ala/acrl/acrlstandards/guidelinesinstruction.htm.

Banta, T. W., Lund, J. P., Black, K. E., & Oblander, F. W. (1996). *Assessment in practice: Putting principles to work on college campuses.* San Francisco: Jossey-Bass (p. 3, 233).

Bodi, S. (2002). How do we bridge the gap between what we teach and what they do? Some thoughts on the place of questions in the process of research. *The Journal of Academic Librarianship, 28*(3), 109-114.

Breivik, P. S., & McDermand, R. (2004). Campus partnerships building on success: A look at San Jose University. *College & Research Libraries News, 65*(4), 210-215.

Brown, G., Bull, J., & Pendlebury, M. (1997). *Assessing student learning in higher education.* London: Routledge.

Cardwell, C. (2001). Faculty: An essential resource for reference librarians. *The Reference Librarian, 73*, 253-263.

Cardwell, C., Furlong, K., & O'Keeffe, J. (2002). My librarian: Personalized research clinics and the academic library. *Research Strategies, 18*(2), 97-111.

Case, D. O. (2002). *Looking for information: A survey of research on information seeking, needs, and behavior.* Amsterdam: Academic Press.

Cunningham, T. H., & Lanning, S. (2002). New frontier trail guides: Faculty-librarian collaboration on information literacy. *Reference Services Review, 30*(4), 343-348.

Elmborg, J. K. (2002). Teaching at the desk: Toward a reference pedagogy. *portal: Libraries and the Academy, 2*(3), 455-464.

Hall, L. (1999). A home-grown program for raising faculty information competence. *Computers in Libraries, 19*(8), 28-34.

Hinchliffe, L. J., & Woodard, B. S. (2001). Instruction. In Bopp, R. E. & L. C. Smith (Eds.). *Reference and information services: An introduction* (3rd ed., pp. 177-209). Englewood, CO: Libraries Unlimited.

Janes, J. (2003). What is reference for? *Reference Services Review, 31*(1), 22-25.

Knight, L. A. (2002). The role of assessment in library user education. *Reference Services Review, 30*(1), 15-24.

Lindauer, B. G. (1998). Defining and measuring the library's impact on campuswide outcomes. *College and Research Libraries, 59*(6), 546-570.

McCord, S. K., & Nofsinger, M. M. (2002). Continuous assessment at Washington State University Libraries: A case study. *Performance Measurement and Metrics, 3*(2), 68-73.

McCutcheon, C., & Lambert, N. M. (2001). Tales untold: The connection between instruction and reference services. *Research Strategies, 18*(3), 203-214.

Mosley, P. A. (1998). Creating a library assignment workshop for university faculty. *The Journal of Academic Librarianship, 24*(1), 33-42.

Neeley, T. Y, Lederer, N., Reyes, A., Thistlethwaite, P., Wess, L., & Winkler, J. (2000). Instruction and outreach at Colorado State University Libraries. *The Reference Librarian, 67/68,* 273-287.

Palomba, C. A., & Banta, T. W. (1999). *Assessment essentials: Planning, implementing and improving assessment in higher education.* San Francisco: Jossey-Bass.

Purdue, J. (2003). Stories, not information: Transforming information literacy. *portal: Libraries and the Academy, 3*(4), 653-662.

Rader, H. B. (2000). Information literacy in the reference environment: Preparing for the future. *The Reference Librarian, 71,* 25-33.

Reeves, L., Nishimuta, C., McMillan, J., & Godin, C. (2003). Faculty outreach: A win-win proposition. *The Reference Librarian, 82,* 57-68.

Rettig, J. (2003). Technology, cluelessness, anthropology, and the Memex: The future of academic reference service. *Reference Services Review, 31*(1), 17-21.

Rockman, I. F. (2002a). Strengthening connections between information literacy, general education, and assessment efforts. *Library Trends, 51*(2), 185-199.

Rockman, I. F. (2002b). The importance of assessment. *Reference Services Review, 30*(3), 181-182.

Saunders, E. S. (2003). The effect of bibliographic instruction on the demand for reference services. *portal: Libraries and the Academy, 3*(1), 35-39.

Westbrook, L., & Tucker, S. A. (2002). Understanding faculty information needs: A process in the context of service. *Reference & User Services Quarterly, 42*(2), 144-148.

Williams, J. L. (2000). Creativity in assessment of library instruction. *Reference Services Review, 28*(4), 323-334.

APPENDIX

The Professional Development Institute Session Evaluation
Office of Instructional Services, Colorado State University

To enhance future PDI planning, please fill out this form at the end of the presentation.

Session: "Find it Fast: Research Tips for People in a Hurry"

Please rate the quality of each of the following:

1. Overall session
   Excellent ___   *Good* ___   *Satisfactory* ___   *Unsatisfactory* ___   *Poor* ___

2. Content presented
   Excellent ___   *Good* ___   *Satisfactory* ___   *Unsatisfactory* ___   *Poor* ___

3. Presenter's delivery of content
   Excellent ___   *Good* ___   *Satisfactory* ___   *Unsatisfactory* ___   *Poor* ___

4. Presenter's knowledge of the topic
   Excellent ___   *Good* ___   *Satisfactory* ___   *Unsatisfactory* ___   *Poor* ___

5. Integration of graphics and/or visual aids
   Excellent ___   *Good* ___   *Satisfactory* ___   *Unsatisfactory* ___   *Poor* ___

6. This session met my professional/personal needs
   Excellent ___   *Good* ___   *Satisfactory* ___   *Unsatisfactory* ___   *Poor* ___

7. I would be interested in attending a follow-up session(s) on this topic
   Excellent ___   *Good* ___   *Satisfactory* ___   *Unsatisfactory* ___   *Poor* ___

8. Future sessions on this topic should be from a perspective outside of CSU
   Excellent ___   *Good* ___   *Satisfactory* ___   *Unsatisfactory* ___   *Poor* ___

9. Comments on the session and/or follow-up sessions (Use back if necessary.)

10. Suggestions for future PDI topics (If you have already listed future topics on another session evaluation form, please do not repeat them on this form.)

Floating and Idea:
Peer Observations Across the Mississippi

Mary Heinzman
David Weaver

SUMMARY. During the 2001-2002 academic year, Augustana College Library (Rock Island, IL) and St. Ambrose University Library (Davenport, IA) began a unique joint venture of peer observation between the reference staff members of the two libraries. Librarians from each college took turns visiting the other library and conducting peer observations of reference desk service. Although the reasons each library had for initiating this venture differed, both libraries benefited from this project. This article discusses the development of the program, the results, and plans for the future. *[Article copies available for a fee from The Haworth Document Delivery Service: 1-800-HAWORTH. E-mail address: <docdelivery@haworthpress.com> Website: <http://www.HaworthPress.com> © 2006 by The Haworth Press, Inc. All rights reserved.]*

KEYWORDS. Academic libraries, college libraries, peer review, reference service

Mary Heinzman is Head of Reference, O'Keefe Library, St. Ambrose University, Davenport, IA 52803 (E-mail: HeinzmanMaryB@sau.edu).

David Weaver is Reference Coordinator, Thomas Tredway Library, Augustana College, Rock Island, IL 61201 (E-mail: alidw@augustana.edu).

[Haworth co-indexing entry note]: "Floating and Idea: Peer Observations Across the Mississippi." Heinzman, Mary, and David Weaver. Co-published simultaneously in *Public Services Quarterly* (The Haworth Information Press, an imprint of The Haworth Press, Inc.) Vol. 2, No. 2/3, 2006, pp. 33-46; and: *Reference Assessment and Evaluation* (ed: Tom Diamond, and Mark Sanders) The Haworth Information Press, an imprint of The Haworth Press, Inc., 2006, pp. 33-46. Single or multiple copies of this article are available for a fee from The Haworth Document Delivery Service [1-800-HAWORTH, 9:00 a.m. - 5:00 p.m. (EST). E-mail address: docdelivery@haworthpress.com].

doi:10.1300/J295v02n02_04

INTRODUCTION

St. Ambrose University, located in Davenport, Iowa, and Augustana College, located in Rock Island, Illinois, are small liberal arts institutions situated on opposite banks of the Mississippi River. St. Ambrose University is an independent Catholic university offering four-year undergraduate programs in the liberal arts, pre-professional and career-oriented programs, and masters and doctoral programs. Approximately 3,500 students attend St. Ambrose University, including many non-traditional students. Augustana College is a private, four-year liberal arts undergraduate college founded by Swedish immigrants with ties to the Evangelical Lutheran Church. Student population is 2,200 at Augustana. Both institutions built new, state-of-the-art libraries in the 1990s. Because of their close proximity, the libraries often participate in shared activities.

The librarians at Augustana College are classified as faculty and must participate in a faculty review process every five years. During the 2001-2002 academic year, the Augustana College Library Director wanted to develop a method of evaluating librarians' abilities at the reference desk and in the classroom for use in the review process.

"Here we are, spending lots of personnel hours on reference, by providing the service and training. Yet, we really did not know too much about how well we were doing it. I hoped the peer evaluation would augment other forms of evaluation (self and user evaluation). However, I did think that this form of evaluation might be more convincing for non-librarian faculty who would see it in the context of the faculty review process than anything I, or the individual librarian, might say in a review document. There were also a lot of concerns about taping reference transactions, or about non-librarians observing interactions, so this seemed to be a relatively non-threatening alternative."

Several factors drove the process of evaluating the librarians, including the fact that the school's Welfare Committee would soon begin reviewing librarians' job performance, the same committee that determines tenure for other faculty and promotion for faculty rank. The Welfare Committee's main charge is to evaluate all full-time and adjunct faculty members at Augustana College and make recommendations to the president of the college in the area of salary, promotion, tenure, and sabbatical leave. Since the librarians at Augustana College are now designated as faculty, they are included in the Welfare Committee's review process. As part of his responsibilities, the Reference Coordinator at Augustana received an assignment to review potential methods of evaluating the librarians.

After research and discussion, the Augustana librarians decided to develop a portfolio for the Welfare Committee review process. The portfolio would be a primary source of information to the Welfare Committee in the evaluation of the librarians. Part of that portfolio would include an evaluation that allowed librarians to demonstrate to faculty members their roles at the reference desk, the classroom, and their daily work responsibilities. The reference desk at Augustana College is staffed not only by the Reference Department librarians, but also by the Technical Services librarian and the Special Collections librarian. Since the librarians perform types of work other than teaching, they were concerned that non-librarian faculty would not know what to assess while evaluating the librarians. Kroll notes that ". . . too often, a campus-wide personnel review panel composed entirely of non-library faculty will expect the tenure dossier of a participating academic librarian to equal in every respect the dossier of a professor of library science" (1983, p. 29). Hill (1994) agrees with this conclusion, stating that it is important that non-librarians, as well as the librarians reviewing tenure and promotion recommendations for library faculty, have an appropriate understanding of librarianship. However, Augustana librarians also believed a peer observation from librarians external to their institution might be helpful. In addition, they felt that the evaluation tools needed to be simple to use, something that allowed librarians to receive feedback on areas where they excelled and areas needing improvement. Required components of the portfolio included a current resume/vita; a 3-6 page personal statement detailing responsibilities, goals, and achievements; copies of relevant handouts, multimedia presentations, bibliographies, etc.; and the annual review by the library director. Optional components included student feedback in the form of completed questionnaires and copies of peer observations conducted by the St. Ambrose University librarians.

The librarians at St. Ambrose University (Davenport, IA) are not classified as faculty and do not participate in the faculty review process, but are nevertheless always looking for ways to improve service. In addition, they appreciate the opportunity to exchange ideas with librarians from other institutions and explore new ways of providing services. They felt that the general results of this joint project with Augustana

College could also be used during the St. Ambrose University accreditation process that is conducted every five years.

Consequently, the reference librarians at the two libraries agreed to work together in a unique peer observation project, one beneficial for both libraries. Although located in different states, the two libraries are only five miles apart, separated by the Mississippi River. Augustana College's academic calendar consists of three 10-week terms, with each term followed by one week designated for final exams. St. Ambrose University follows the more traditional 16-week semester calendar. Thus, the "busy" times for the libraries are often different. Librarians believed that the alternate schedules would help facilitate the observation process.

LITERATURE REVIEW

In reviewing literature assessing library reference service, many assessments measure the accuracy of answers to specific questions (Bailey, 1987), or the numbers of questions answered. Fewer assess the service behaviors and communication skills of reference librarians. Although accuracy of answers is an important component of reference service, it should not be the only indicator of quality service. Bicknell (1994) suggests that staff behaviors and user needs/expectations should also be considered. Aluri and Reichel suggest that in "institutions where librarians have faculty status and are subject to the review process, counting of publications and service activities is an easier evaluation method than assessment of job performance" (1994, p. 148). Furthermore, they state that one problem with internal peer evaluation is that the evaluator is often competing for the same promotion and/or raise. Wallace and Van Fleet (2001) assert that a librarian's interviewing, listening, and approachability skills are also indicators of a successful reference transaction. One of the case studies they present concludes that not all behaviors are exhibited all of the time, and advocates the use of a checklist during unobtrusive observation of reference service as one way to measure successful service.

In 2003, the Reference User Services Association's (RUSA) Task Force on Professional Competencies developed a model statement of competencies essential for successful reference service librarians. Among the competencies defined are responsiveness to user needs, critical thinking, communication skills, and developing relationships with colleagues and users. The Committee states that "Many aspects of the information service interaction are intangible and difficult to measure objectively" (2003, p. 294). Bicknell's article suggests ways to measure communication skills and behaviors and goes on to say that "combining two or more evaluation techniques may be most successful for assessing communication skills and behaviors" (1994, p. 79). Murfin (1995) also suggests that the best evaluation of reference success will use multiple methods of evaluation. Hernon and Dugan state that "assessment should not ignore user perceptions of service quality and satisfaction" (2002, p. 131). They suggest the use of several survey instruments that measure service quality, including such factors as empathy, responsiveness, knowledge, and courtesy of librarians.

Radford (1998) examines the role of nonverbal communication in the academic library, but does not address other behaviors. Radford concludes that "the reference encounter is not exclusively task oriented, focusing exclusively on the exchange of information, as often portrayed in the library literature" (p. 714). She goes on to suggest that the role of nonverbal communication in the reference encounter needs more study. Rice-Lively and Racine (1997) also explore the expanding role of academic librarians and note that librarians must be good communicators, interpreters, and listeners. Whitlatch (2000) agrees that the assessment of reference service involves the impact of nonverbal communication, the user's willingness to return, librarians' behaviors, and the interpersonal dynamics between librarian and user. Keeping these things in mind, the librarians at St. Ambrose University and Augustana College developed the following process.

METHODOLOGY

The Augustana librarians determined that part of their faculty review process would include the development of a multi-component portfolio. The portfolio's components, some required and some optional, demonstrated to the Welfare Committee the types of responsibilities and tasks that each librarian performed. Two of the optional survey instruments in the portfolio include a service questionnaire and observation of service provided. In order to make the observations as objective as possible, staff members suggested that having peers from outside Augustana College, yet from a similar environment (small liberal arts college) served as the best possible choice. It would legitimize to non-librarian faculty the observations, as well as articulate some of the goals of the reference interaction. This could also be seen as a learning opportunity for librarians in an objective yet non-threatening environment. The librarians conducting the observation would not be competing with those being observed for the same promotions, raises, and tenure.

Optional components in the portfolio indicative of reference service quality included: (1) evaluations completed by the Reference Coordinator and another randomly selected Augustana reference librarian; (2) the results of a service questionnaire distributed to students and faculty receiving reference service; and (3) peer observations performed by two St. Ambrose University librarians.

The Reference Coordinator at Augustana College and the Head of Reference at St. Ambrose University met to discuss the concept of peer observation between the two institutions. They initially developed a set of standards, or behaviors to observe, based on those mentioned by Whitlatch (2000). After developing a draft list of reference behaviors, librarians from the two libraries met as a group, discussed the list, and provided input. Their suggestions helped in revising the checklist; each librarian received a revised copy (see Table 1).

The two supervisors met again to set up a schedule for library visits. Initially, two different librarians from St. Ambrose University observe the same Augustana librarian at separate times, and then individually summarize the observations. St. Ambrose University librarians participated voluntarily, and the initial schedule during the trial period had three of the four reference librarians scheduled to observe at Augustana College. When possible, observation times coincided with the perceived busiest times at the reference desk. An established minimum observation time of two hours created an excellent overall picture of the service provided. Each St. Ambrose University librarian possessed several copies of the observation checklist to use during the observation period, with the idea being that a separate checklist would be used for each reference transaction. After the observation periods, the St. Ambrose University librarians compiled independent summaries of their visits. They forwarded their summaries to the Reference Coordinator at Augustana, to be shared as appropriate with the librarians being observed. Shortly after this initial observation period, three librarians from Augustana scheduled to come to St. Ambrose University to observe and write summaries of their observations.

After the initial round of peer observations, the supervisors met to revise the observation checklist and to determine if another round of observations would be appropriate. Several librarians felt that the checklist served only as a guide, since not every transaction involved all aspects of the checklist. Other librarians felt that the items on the check-

TABLE 1. Peer Review Checklist

Peer Review of: _____   Date: _____

Approachability, Comfort, and Interest:

___ Smiles	___ Is mobile, goes with patron	___ Makes attentive comments
___ Makes eye contact	___ Shows relaxed body posture	___ Speaks in interested tone
___ Friendly verbal greeting	___ Gives patron full attention	

Comments:

Negotiation (Inquiry):   Teaching:

___ Asks open questions	___ Directs student to take control of research in some way
___ Probes	(has student keyboard, manipulate mouse, etc.)
___ Paraphrases/clarifies	___ Introduces student to (and explains) specific search
___ Informs	technique
___ Summarizes	___ Asks guided/leading questions, challenges student to think
___ Uses common language	___ Explains how and why the information is organized
	___ Supports student's creative questions

Comments:

Tools/Resources:

___ Introduces student to appropriate resource (and explains why)
___ Presents several choices/possibilities/options for student
___ Fully understands resource(s) and is able to explain strengths and limitations to student

Comments:

Follow Up:

___ Asks "Does this answer your question?" (or something similar)
___ Closes the interview tactfully and/or invites later assistance

Comments:

What did I learn? _____
What did I share? _____

Observer: _____   Time: _____

list did not capture the essence of the reference transaction. In retrospect, the librarians found it useful to understand the reference transaction checklist on paper before observing, so that they could look at the reference interview in a more objective manner. The participating librarians felt that one of the key components of this project turned out to be the opportunity to learn from each other. In most cases, the learning revolved around different communication techniques, unusual searching techniques or methodologies, and the use of new reference resources. After input from all the librarians, the checklist received an upgrade with new sections titled "What I learned" and "What I shared" added at the end. Each observation summary completed also included the new sections. Keeping that in mind, the Augustana librarians also had the option to include the results of a user survey, in addition to the peer observations in their portfolios submitted for the faculty review process (see Table 2). If a librarian chose to include the user survey component in the portfolio, she must include results of all surveys returned, both positive and negative. This survey asked questions about the user's perception of the service received.

The librarian providing the reference service circled his/her initials at the top of the survey before handing it out at the end of the reference transaction. The main goal served to provide a means of assessing each librarian individually, instead of the reference department as a whole. Questionnaires could be returned to boxes located near the library exits. Augustana's Reference Coordinator compiled and shared the results only with each individual librarian. The questionnaire asked both quantitative and qualitative questions. Based on Dewdney and Ross' article (1994), the most important question asked users if, in the end, they would return to a librarian for assistance in the future.

During the initial observation period, patrons returned 188 questionnaires, and the Reference Coordinator recorded the results. Due to the scheduling of the reference desk, the four librarians whose main responsibility is reference work received the most responses. One librarian received a score of 66, the highest number returned; another received a score of 4, the lowest number returned. Each librarian received a sheet listing the overall library average for each question, as well as their individual averages. In this way, the librarians easily noted if their average score ranked above or below the overall library average. Responses to Question 7 provided the best score for the librarians as a whole: Would you return to this librarian for assistance in the future? Based on a scale of 1 being the highest value score, and 4 being the lowest score, this question received an overall average of 1.02. The lowest average score,

TABLE 2. Reference Desk Services Questionnaire

Please help us evaluate the quality of our reference desk services. On the four point scales, circle the number that best represents your opinion. Place the completed survey in one of the boxes located next to the library exits.

1. Did the librarian make you feel welcome and comfortable?

very welcome and comfortable   1 : 2 : 3 : 4   very unwelcome and uncomfortable

Comments:

2. What did you learn from the librarian that may be useful in the future?

3. The interaction with the librarian was:

very useful   1 : 2 : 3 : 4   not at all useful

4. At the end of the interview, how well did the librarian understand your question?

completely   1 : 2 : 3 : 4   not at all

5. After assistance from the librarian, was/were your question(s) answered?

6. Overall, how satisfied were you with the assistance provided by the librarian?

very satisfied   1 : 2 : 3 : 4   not at all satisfied

7. Would you return to this librarian for assistance in the future?

yes   probably   probably not   no

Please complete the following information (circle one):

1. Augustana student / Augustana faculty / Augustana staff / Augustana alumni / Quad Cities Grad Center Student / High School Student / Other College student / Other

2. If Augustana student, what year? 1st / 2nd / 3rd / 4th

3. Male / Female

1.09 for Question 4, indicates that the reference librarians as a whole should focus more on listening, paraphrasing, and determining the actual reference question (see Table 3). Augustana students completed 91% of all returned questionnaires. Faculty, staff, or the general public completed the remainder of the surveys. Librarians received encouragement to include these scores in their portfolios.

PROBLEMS

Because Augustana College is on a trimester schedule while St. Ambrose University is on a semester schedule, both schools hoped that the librarian received more opportunities to observe during busy times at the other facility. In reality, it did not work out that way during the first round of observations. The times when a librarian from one college was available to observe often occurred during a slow time at the other institution. As a result, some peer observations included a very limited

TABLE 3. Results of Reference Desk Services Questionnaire

Librarian	Q1	Q3	Q4	Q6	Q7	Number Returned
L1 Average	1.02	1.08	1.12	1.06	1.00	66
L2 Average	1.00	1.00	1.00	1.00	1.00	4
L3 Average	1.15	1.15	1.11	1.05	1.15	20
L4 Average	1.00	1.00	1.00	1.00	1.00	5
L5 Average	1.00	1.00	1.17	1.17	1.00	6
L6 Average	1.06	1.09	1.08	1.07	1.02	47
L7 Average	1.07	1.00	1.00	1.00	1.00	31
L8 Average	1.22	1.00	1.00	1.22	1.00	9
Grand Average	1.06	1.07	1.09	1.07	1.02	188

number of reference transactions, while others had numerous service opportunities to observe.

The process of transferring the completed observations from one institution to another proved cumbersome, since a report needed to be completed and shared with two Reference supervisors, and then relayed to the individual librarian. In order for the observation summaries to be appropriate for inclusion in the Augustana Library portfolios, the summaries needed to be signed and dated by Augustana's Reference Coordinator. Not being a requirement necessary for the observation summaries of the St. Ambrose librarians, the two schools eliminated this step for summaries going to St. Ambrose University. This process will have to be reevaluated if St. Ambrose University decides to formalize librarians' review process.

Another problem is that, while the missions for service at the reference desk are very similar, in actual practice there are differences in philosophy and many things are open for interpretation. For example, one librarian's "teaching opportunity" differs from another librarian. One librarian will be more patient, encouraging the student to struggle with a failed search, while the other librarian does not want to waste time on a search that will not yield relevant results. The observing librarian may consider this either a "lost" teaching opportunity, or an efficient way of handling the situation depending on his/her philosophy of service.

Another difficulty is that the observer often is unaware of the nature of the relationship between librarian and student. For example, the librarians at St. Ambrose University teach a one-credit hour information literacy course and often develop good working relationships with many students. The St. Ambrose University librarian will often know the classes and assignments for the students they are assisting. While this is useful during the interaction between the student and librarian, it makes observation more difficult since the observer has to make many assumptions. Does the librarian already know what the information needs are for an assignment or is she assuming she knows?

The portfolios compiled by the Augustana librarians presented another concern. At the project's onset, the portfolio included specific required components and three possible optional components. Each librarian could decide whether to include the optional components in his/her individual portfolio. This setup occurred partly because of one librarian's initial resistance. The librarian wanted to see what the final product looked like before agreeing to include it in his/her portfolio. Since this served as the inaugural event for peer observations and that the library director wanted everyone to participate, the review process allowed individual librarians to choose the components. However, this resulted in some librarians having more extensive portfolios than others.

Also, the time factor served as an important issue. To make this a successful project, the directors at both libraries allowed librarians time to devote to observing and writing reports. However, the participating librarians already had numerous other responsibilities; they needed to be well-organized and flexible in order to make this work. One possible solution to the time issue is to make peer observation just a part of the regular reference desk schedule, assigning dates and times to complete the observations.

OUTCOMES

At the end of the first year of observations, the participating librarians took part in an informal survey as to their opinions about the project. A list of the questions asked is listed in Table 4. The majority of the librarians felt that the project's greatest benefit offered the chance to network and interact with librarians from another institution. One librarian said, "I learned a great deal about their teaching methods, interactions with faculty, and how they market their library that I have found to be helpful here in my library." Another librarian thought "it would be great if all of the librarians that participated sat down together to discuss improving reference–not just the individual transactions, but overall changes, new approaches, etc." One librarian felt that the observations "forced me to re-evaluate what I do at the reference and why I do it. In any service occupation there exists a danger of falling into a rut." Overall, the participating librarians felt that this was a very positive, worthwhile project. Fritch and Mandernack comment that "Exchanging librarians and reference staff members. . . .can be extremely productive in a complex and changing information environment. Learning new resources (both print and electronic), interacting with different user groups, and gaining exposure to new techniques, approaches, and organizational structures are just some of the benefits of such a program" (2001, p. 302). This project seems to corroborate their statement.

The project allowed the librarians from each institution to get to know each other better and provided opportunities to collaborate on other projects. This year, the librarians are discussing ways to expand this project to include peer observation of information literacy instruction and classroom techniques. St. Ambrose University has a one-credit hour information literacy course that all new students are required to

TABLE 4. Follow-Up Questions for Librarians

1. Do you feel this peer observation has been worthwhile? Why or why not?

2. How has this peer observation helped your reference service?

3. Did peer observation have a negative impact on the reference transaction? (creating nervousness on your part, student inhibited in asking questions, etc.)

4. Would you be interested in continuing this project?

5. If so, what suggestions would you make to improve this project?

6. What impact or changes, if any, did this project bring to you or your library?

take and Augustana College is working with faculty to include information literacy components into several core classes. Expanding the observation to instruction techniques would help the librarians develop their teaching skills. Once again, time is an important issue to consider, so peer observation of instruction might have to be limited to either certain individuals, or to certain times of the year.

Other "bonus" benefits of this project include sharing ideas about marketing the library, suggestions for displays and exhibits, and ideas for new services that could be offered to faculty and students. Richardson notes "Learning, then, it would seem, almost naturally happens through peer observation. The unique benefit of observation is that it provides a forum for learning through exposure, contemplation, and often, imitation" (2000, p. 13). The librarians at Augustana College and St. Ambrose University agree that this is perhaps the project's greatest benefit.

REFERENCES

Aluri, R., & Reichel, M. (1994). Performance evaluation: A deadly disease? *The Journal of Academic Librarianship, 20*(3), 145-155.

Bailey, B. (1987). The "55 percent rule" revisited. *The Journal of Academic Librarianship, 13*(5), 280-282.

Bicknell, T. (1994). Focusing on quality reference service. *The Journal of Academic Librarianship, 20*(2), 77-81.

Dewdney, P., & Ross, C. (1994). Flying a light aircraft: Reference service evaluation from a user's viewpoint. *RQ, 34*(2), 217-230.

Fritch, J. W., & Mandernack, S. B. (2001). The emerging reference paradigm: A vision of reference services in a complex information environment. *Library Trends, 50*(2), 286-305.

Hernon, P., & Dugan, R. (2002). *An action plan for outcomes assessment in your library.* Chicago: American Library Association.

Hill, J. S. (1994). Wearing our own clothes: Librarians as faculty. *The Journal of Academic Librarianship, 20*(2), 71-76.

Kroll, H. R. (1983). Beyond evaluation: Performance appraisal as a planning and motivational tool in libraries. *The Journal of Academic Librarianship, 9*(1), 27-32.

Murfin, M. E. (1995). Evaluation of reference service by user report of success. *The Reference Librarian, 49/50*, 229-241.

Radford, M. L. (1998). Approach or avoidance? The role of nonverbal communication in the academic library user's decision to initiate a reference encounter. *Library Trends, 46*(4), 699-717.

Rice-Lively, M. L., & Racine, J. D. (1997). The role of academic librarians in the era of information technology. *The Journal of Academic Librarianship, 23*(1), 31-41.

Richardson, M. O. (2000). Peer observation: Learning from one another. *Thought & Action: The NEA Higher Education Journal, 16*(1), 9-20.

RUSA Task Force on Professional Competencies. (2003). Professional competencies for reference and user services librarians. *Reference & User Services Quarterly, 42*(4), 290-295. Also available at www.ala.org/ala/rusa/rusaprotocols/referenceguide/profesisonal.htm.

Wallace, D., & Van Fleet, C. (2001). *Library evaluation: A casebook and can-do guide.* Englewood, CO: Libraries Unlimited.

Whitlatch, J. B. (2000). *Evaluating reference services: A practical guide.* Chicago: American Library Association.

Merged Reference Desks in a Merged Library Environment: The Impact of Merging Government Publications

Susan L. Kendall

Lorene R. Sisson

SUMMARY. A new library in San José opened on August 1, 2003. This library is the result of a unique collaboration between San José State University Library and the San José Public Library. The planning for this new library highlighted merging several key areas of operation, including Government Publications. Several years before the two libraries merged, the University Library merged government publications reference functions into the general reference service of the Reference department. Depository library status at the federal and state levels impacted the planning and implementation stages. This paper discusses the background, planning, and implementation of merging the reference service for government publications, first within an academic environment and then in the unique joint library environment. *[Article copies available for a fee from The Haworth Document Delivery Service: 1-800-HAWORTH. E-mail address: <docdelivery@haworthpress.com> Website: <http://www.HaworthPress.com> © 2006 by The Haworth Press, Inc. All rights reserved.]*

Susan L. Kendall is Coordinator of Government Publications (E-mail: susan. kendall@sjsu.edu); and Lorene R. Sisson is Reference and Instruction Librarian (E-mail: lorene.sisson@sjsu.edu), both at San José State University Library, San José, CA 95192-0028.

[Haworth co-indexing entry note]: "Merged Reference Desks in a Merged Library Environment: The Impact of Merging Government Publications." Kendall, Susan L., and Lorene R. Sisson. Co-published simultaneously in *Public Services Quarterly* (The Haworth Information Press, an imprint of The Haworth Press, Inc.) Vol. 2, No. 2/3, 2006, pp. 47-67; and: *Reference Assessment and Evaluation* (ed: Tom Diamond, and Mark Sanders) The Haworth Information Press, an imprint of The Haworth Press, Inc., 2006, pp. 47-67. Single or multiple copies of this article are available for a fee from The Haworth Document Delivery Service [1-800-HAWORTH, 9:00 a.m. - 5:00 p.m. (EST). E-mail address: docdelivery@haworthpress.com].

doi:10.1300/J295v02n02_05

KEYWORDS. Reference, government publications, Federal Library Depository Program, mergers, academic libraries, public libraries

INTRODUCTION

A new library in San José opened on August 1, 2003, the result of a merger between San José State University Library (SJSU) and the San José Public Library (SJPL). Before this merger took place, SJSU Library had completed a major reorganization. The SJSU Library accomplished several mergers of service points, including merging government publications into the reference department. This experience helped to prepare the university librarians and staff for the merger of the two very distinct library organizations.

Collaborative, collegial creativity is a necessity in providing reference services in a tough fiscal environment. The merged reference service project is an example of the dynamic and innovative nature of the two libraries. The SJSU Library serves as a vital and integral part of the university campus. Librarians participate in governance, curriculum, and the scholarly life of the University. The Library's mission and goals are aligned with the University. Growth of the local community brought opportunities and challenges to the university community over the years. The University's location in the downtown community of San José involved the University with the city's regional development issues. This resulted in substantial benefits for both communities. San José is one of the three largest cities in California. It is considered to be the capital of Silicon Valley, headquarters for cutting edge technology and creative, innovative entrepreneurs.

LITERATURE REVIEW

The merging of government publications departments with reference departments appeared frequently in the literature during the 1990s. The literature reveals several factors, internal and external, that caused these reorganizations. Vice President Gore's 1993 initiative to migrate federal publications to a digital environment is discussed in Aldrich (2002). This migration had major implications for libraries that participated in the Federal Depository Library Program (FDLP). Discussions concerning the future of the FDLP have continued and expanded to discussions of the necessity for separate government publications departments in libraries. Pre-dating the Gore initiative, Hernon and McClure (1988) wrote on accessing government information. This classic work on government publications pinpoints issues concerning integrating government information resources with the reference department. Successful integration relies on in-depth planning and evaluation of services. Once these are in place, issues such as professional development, physical location, bibliographic control, organizational control, and marketing are more rationally resolved. Kinder (1991) also pre-dates the Gore initiative, but contains background information that impacted the merging of government documents reference service. In the late 1980s and early 1990s, the Government Printing Office (GPO) loaded bibliographic records in OCLC and online catalogs with keyword access appeared in many libraries.

Planning, accessing, and training remain a constant concern today as in 1991. Amata (1996) reported on an ALA conference workshop that included several papers on the issues concerning reorganization in the mid-1990s. Several common threads ran through these presentations, including the need for administrative support, the accessibility of bibliographic records, the necessity of planning for government publications and the entire reference service, and the need for continual training. Wilhoit (2000) reported on a later ALA conference that featured the merger of government publications and reference services. This conference report targeted the factors that led to mergers. Factors included institution budget cuts, renovation of the library, growing awareness of government publications as a resource, loading bibliographic information into the online catalog, the desire to consolidate like services, and the need for thorough planning and training. Frazer (1997) discusses an actual merger at Old Dominion University (ODU). The merger removed artificial boundaries between reference and government publications. The reasons for the merger are similar to ones stated by Amata and Wilhoit. However, ODU faced the retirement of the head of government publications, which impacted the planning for the merger. Once completed, the merger presented ODU with the problem of ensuring the continued success of the reference department in handling government publications questions. Farrell (2000) lists the advantages of merging government publications with a reference department, such as having one central reference service point, integrating government documents into the overall collection development decisions, and including government documents as reference tools. Farrell also comments about the complexity of government documents and the need for training.

Complexity in government publications reference service is further discussed in Taylor and Schmidt (2001). Colorado State University (CStU) merged the Government Publications Department with Social Sciences, Humanities and Science Reference Services in 1996. With bibliographic records added into the online catalog, patrons can see the library's recent holdings of government publications without asking the librarian for help. However, not all of the government publications are in the catalog and accessing much of the collection is a complex task. Ongoing training is the key quality reference service. CStU assigns a librarian to serve as the specialist for government publications, just as there is a librarian for subject specialties. King (2003) reported on the need for continued collegial communications in reference departments even in such mundane tasks as scheduling. All of these authors refer to the importance of planning, evaluating, and training in developing a successful merged reference service.

BACKGROUND

San José State University

San José State University (SJSU), established in 1857, is the oldest public institution of higher education on the west coast. The school began in San Francisco as Minn's Evening Normal School to train teachers. The school was renamed the California Normal School in 1862, when it became the first state funded institution of higher education in California.

In 1870, the Normal School moved to San José. By 1961, San José Normal School had become San José State College and joined the California State University System (CSU). The CSU system is currently one of the larger college systems in the United States, with 23 individual campuses and over 408,000 students. In 1962, the college library was designated a federal depository, the only one located in San José. The college name changed in 1974 to San José State University. SJSU continues to grow with current enrollment at approximately 26,000 students, nearly 1,700 faculty, and offers over 134 different bachelor and master degree programs (San José State University, 2004).

The University and the CSU system encourage unique and creative collaborative efforts. Creative collaborative ventures at SJSU have included partnerships with the business community, other academic institutions, and local government. Examples include doctoral programs in education and engineering within the University of California system and the CSU system. In fact, the current mission statement of SJSU begins with these words, "In collaboration with nearby industries and communities. . . ." The merger of the University Library with the San José Public Library marks one of the largest projects exemplifying this concept of collaboration.

San José Public Library

Founded in 1777 by Spanish explorers, the city of San José served as California's first state capital in 1849. In 1880, taxpayers established the first official city tax-supported library. Over the next few decades, the size of the collections increased, which created a need for a new library building. In 1903 San José opened a Carnegie-funded library on what is now the site of the new King Library. By the 1930s, the public library needed more space for its expanding collections. The San José Public Library was moved into the former post office building in downtown San José. In 1936, the University purchased the Carnegie building and site. From 1937 to 1970, the city library remained in the former post office building. A bond issue and federal grants enabled the city to start construction of a new library building. In 1970, the new main public library for the city of San José opened a few blocks away from the university campus (San José State Public Libraries and San José State University Library, 2003).

The City Library currently includes 17 branches, with plans to add six new sites and expand 14 of the branch libraries. The City Library serves a population of 924,950 with a budget of $26.5 million. The Library system owns nearly 2 million items. The current mission of the San José Public Library states: "San José Public Library enriches lives by fostering lifelong learning and by ensuring that every member of the community has access to a vast array of ideas and information."

MERGING SERVICE POINTS AT SJSU CLARK LIBRARY

In February 1997, the SJSU Academic Priority Steering Committee's *Preliminary Academic Priorities Report* endorsed "the Library's efforts to produce cost efficiencies through consolidation of service points, space rearrangements, etc." The Government Publications reference desk is one of the service points identified by the library administration. The library administration created the University Library Merge Committee to study this proposed change. This Committee explored the existing academic programs and determined what changes might be appropriate in the number and type of degrees offered.

The University Library Merge Committee Report listed the following factors as elements in favor of merging Government Publications into the Reference department: the reference desks in both departments provided similar services; some reference librarians received training to work at the Government Publications reference desk; the reduction in the reference service hours for Government Publications, thus, a merger of the two desks would restore the service hours; integrating Government Publications resources into the reference desk area would result in their wider visibility and more effective use, and would improve support for other subject areas in the Reference collection; cross training of the integrated staff would result in improved reference skills as reference staff became conversant with Government Publications sources. Eventually, the Government Publications merger would serve as a model for other service point merges. It is interesting to note that Frazer writes, "Moreover, merging public services for government information with the libraries other public service activities removes an artificial boundary based solely on the publisher of a particular resource" (Frazer, 1997, p. 100).

Prior to merging, the Government Publications Department operated similarly to a special library. Located on a different floor from the Reference department, the Government Publications Department's associated collections were shelved in Superintendent of Documents classification order on the same floor as the Government Publications reference desk. This necessitated a separate card catalog for government publications because the Library's online catalog did not provide access to the vast majority of older government publications. However, in 1995, the Library contracted with Marcive to add current government publications bibliographic records to the online catalog.

Government Publications' personnel included two full-time librarians, three full-time support staff, and student workers. The department also utilized librarians interested in learning about government publications and not assigned to the department in helping to cover the department's reference desk service hours. The Government Publications reference desk service hours matched the Reference desk service hours. The Head of Government Publications supervised all aspects of the unit's operation and reported to the library dean. Department personnel managed technical services operations such as acquisitions, catalog maintenance, and all aspects of shelving of government publications.

The Library developed a plan to merge the reference functions of the Government Publications Department into the Reference Department. The technical services aspects of Government Publications merged into the Technical Services Department. To accomplish this change in reference service, librarians and support staff needed a major professional development training program.

THE NEED FOR PROFESSIONAL DEVELOPMENT

The librarians in the Reference and Government Publications departments agreed that reference service for government publications is often complex, time consuming, and confusing. At the time of this first merger, few government publications had migrated to the Internet. Finding government information required knowledge of and the ability to use unique finding tools.

One of the challenges of government publications reference service is locating the desired items, most of which are not easily located through standard library tools or methods. Most SJSU Library materials, other than government publications, generally could be located through the online catalog. Library users could browse the shelves in hopes of serendipitously finding a book on their topic in the appropriate Library of Congress (LC) subject call number area. However, to identify and locate government publications, librarians and patrons must use the government publications card catalog or other specialized reference tools. Browsing the shelves, as is possible in LC, does not work effectively in government publications. Materials are arranged by issuing agency, not by subject. While agencies publish material in their main field of responsibility, they also publish material that might be considered outside that area of responsibility. An example of this is the National School Lunch Program. Those not familiar with the arrangement of government publications might assume that the Department of Education is responsible for this program and all of its publications, but in fact, the school lunch program is a part of the Department of Agriculture.

Another challenge is the various formats found in government publications make shelf browsing difficult. The item sought might be, for example, one single sheet, multiple volumes, CD-ROM, or microfiche. Browsing the collection becomes an inefficient option. The Government Publications reference desk provided in-depth assistance with its specially trained staff.

While the online catalog contained entries for a few of the commonly used items, such as the *Statistical Abstract of the United States*, patrons needed to use the Monthly Catalog (MoCat) or its CD-ROM version to locate pre-1995 publications. Eventually, the MoCat became available on the Internet through GPO Access. The online version of MoCat indexes materials back to 1976. Also, Internet access during its early days proved frustratingly slow, especially when searching for government agencies and their publications. Patrons faced a challenge in having to use the paper version of MoCat to locate pre-1976 materials.

After a patron found a government publication in the MoCat, the patron and Documents staff needed to determine whether the library owned the material. As a partial federal depository, determining actual holdings of particular items is complicated. If the item appeared in the MoCat, this necessitated a second step of checking the Government Publications card catalog to verify receipt of the item. The card catalog, physically located in the government publications area, served a dual role: as a catalog of items by agency and as a shelf list for the department. Once confirmed as being available at the library, the item's location and format needed to be determined. The paper publications are usually straightforward; however, the microfiche items are not shelved with the paper items and had a location code that was somewhat difficult to decipher. Items requiring the use of a computer proved difficult because of the nebulous instructions for using the software. Microopaque format is difficult to read and impossible to photocopy. The shelving and use of these items required specially trained staff working in Government Publications. These complexities, unique features, and formats of government publications required the development of a dedicated professional development plan.

Professional Development Plan in the First Merger

Librarians, staff, and administration recognized the need for a program of professional development in government publications reference service. In addition, the literature supported the view that professional development is the key. As Hernon and McClure stated, "Competent staff that are knowledgeable about government information resources, and have professional attitudes regarding the provision of information services for these materials, are essential if the overall quality of library information services is to be improved" (Hernon & McClure, 1984, p. 219).

The librarians and staff of the Government Publications Department designed a professional development plan for the entire Reference Department. The administration supported this plan by hiring a part-time librarian to help with developing the workshops, scheduling rooms for the sessions, making flyers, and coordinating the details of the sessions. The knowledge of the specific research needs at SJSU contributed to the development of the program. The Government Publications staff reviewed courses that frequently required the use of government information and the most frequent reference questions. They designed a program of five sessions, each one to two hours in length. The first session focused on an overview of the basics of government publications. Topics included finding aids for government publications, GPO Access to the Catalog of U.S. Publications, the web page for the library's government publications, and how to find a government publication in the Clark Library. The session included a written assignment that helped the reference librarians review the material covered.

The next three sessions covered the frequently occurring government publications reference questions. Session two, "Social Policy and Finding U.S. laws," covered online sources such as THOMAS (thomas. loc.gov) and paper sources such as the *U.S. Code, Statutes at Large*, Congressional Information Service publications, and the *Catalog of Federal Domestic Assistance*. This session included written exercises. Session three, "Census and Statistics," covered these major resources. Session four, "California," covered the frequently used state information sources such as *California Legislation, California Code of Regulations*, and tax materials. Session five covered many of the sources not covered in the other sessions such as sources for country information, executive orders, and the federal budget.

The staff taught the sessions the semester before the merger. Also, reference librarians spent time at the Government Publications reference service desk "shadowing" the Government Publications staff. During this time, the Government Publications personnel and Reference department communicated extensively with each other. This communication helped develop the skills needed in the next merger with the public library.

MERGING THE SJSU LIBRARY AND CITY LIBRARY

Around the time that the SJSU library merged reference functions, the mayor of San José, Susan Hammer, and the president of SJSU, Dr. Robert Caret, in one of their regular meetings, discussed their concerns about their respective libraries. Both libraries faced space constraints, new technology demands, and a general need for renovation. SJSU used two buildings, Wahlquist and Clark, for library collections and services. San José had an old facility long in need of enlargement. Both the University and city faced skyrocketing building and real estate costs, preventing the purchase of land for a library to meet their respective needs. In addition, the city's major convention center construction project needed the space the current city library occupied. Both organizations knew the growing need for a new library and desired an innovative and practical solution. Both leaders discussed an innovative solution of the new facility: the merging of the public and university reference desks.

In May 1998, the City of San José and the Trustees of the California State University on behalf of San José State University signed the *Agreement for Ownership and Operation of Joint Library Building and Grant of Easement* document. This led to the establishment of planning teams to accomplish the merger. In March 1999, the Library completed an internal working document, *Strategic Operational Plan for the San José Joint Library*. This unpublished document outlined the strategic plan for work to be completed "for each of the five categories of library operations" (San José State University, 1998, p. 7). Mid-2003 served as the target date to complete the new library. This allowed four years to bring together two unique cultures, separate bureaucracies, and complex organizational structures into a new, unique organization to serve the entire community. SJSU's merging of government publications with reference served as a pilot project in combining two distinct entities. Insights from this experience include the need for extensive planning, communication, and training.

Planning Teams

In March 2000, the Core Planning Team, made up of administrators from both libraries, formed five Joint Operational Task Force teams. Each institution appointed a leader to serve as a co-leader for each team. These co-leaders reported back to the Core Planning Team. User Services, Collections Management, Communications & Cultural Change, On-Line Systems & Technology, and Policies & Procedures (an additional team was established later for Administrative Services) comprised the five-joint planning teams. The co-team leaders attended a two-day project management workshop. Sub-teams created under each team received assignments for specific areas of concern. Each sub-team's charge included gathering large amounts of data such as the current operations of both libraries and similar operations as found in the professional literature. All this information fed into making informed recommendations which were submitted to the main teams. Later, the main teams made these recommendations to the Core Team. The User Services team and the Collections Management team primarily served the government publications interests.

A sub-team for reference services that reported to the User Services team discussed reference services in terms of a merged reference unit. The merged reference unit would consist of the public library reference desk and the university library reference desk that now included government publications reference. Several factors supported the inclusion of government publications in reference. The University Library already had merged government publications into their general reference service. In addition, both institutions served as state depository libraries. As Farrell notes, "The growth of government information on the Internet is another contributing factor in main streaming government information" (Farrell, 2000, p. 11). Meetings identified 19 operational, functional, and philosophical issues relating to reference service. After some discussion, the group established a joint Government Publications sub-team that reported to the Collections Management team and communicated with all other teams (see Appendix 1).

Issues

The Government Publications sub-team examined major issues for government publications reference service in the new library, including which classification system should be used in the Reference area. Depository items had been reclassified from Superintendent of Documents (SuDocs) into the LC Classification System when they were moved to the Reference Department in the SJSU Library. The public library's California state documents and general reference collection were classified in the Dewey Decimal System. The Reference Services and Government Publications sub-teams both recommended to the User Services and the Collections Management teams that all reference materials be classed into the LC Classification System. The two sub-teams forwarded this recommendation to the Core Team.

The second issue concerned circulation of government publications. This new, merged library generally intended to make materials more available to both the university community and the public community. The SJSU Library's role as a federal and state depository obligated it to make government publications available to all. The sub-team recommended that government publications continue to be added to the catalog and available for circulation whenever possible.

A third issue involved determining the location of the circulating government publications items. In the SJSU Clark Library, the second floor near the Government Publications reference desk housed the majority of government publications. The size of the collection and the need to place collections with similar service needs together precluded a location with the reference desk in the new King Library. The Core Team determined that the collection would be housed in the lower level on compact shelving.

The complex nature of government publications and the difficulties in locating items meant that reference librarians and staff needed extensive training in the new King Library. In order to accommodate the extensive planning required for this project, the libraries reviewed procedures necessary to continue daily operations. The libraries reduced or eliminated any tasks, activities, functions, or reports not considered essential for daily operations. For example, SJSU Library suspended annual reports and other statistical record keeping during this labor-intensive project.

To encourage collegiality, each library location alternately hosted planning meetings for the sub-teams. The sub-teams spent time gathering information, discussing the information, analyzing the potential impact, and developing and making recommendations on numerous issues. In addition to the recommendations, the sub-teams developed policy and procedure proposals. In the Reference Services sub-team alone, there were 19 sections, each having sub-sections and details needing to be reviewed. To add to the complexity of this planning process, the sub-teams needed to select an integrated online library system to function and serve both libraries in a seamless manner.

In the process of this planning, statistical data compiled from previous years helped in defining future needs. An integral part of the planning process included Reference service and circulation statistics for government publications. The statistics included in this article give some useful information and perspective on this process.

Statistics

Circulation statistics for government publications in Clark Library, like many institutions, reflected a gradual decline in use. The Government Publications Department manually recorded the circulation activity statistics for paper government publications prior to the first merger. After the first merger in 1999, the circulation system automatically recorded these statistics. As of 2003, use of SJSU government publications subject web pages is recorded. Beginning in August 2004, actual use of electronic government publications has been tracked.

In Table 1, the first and second sets of statistics reflect a general decline in paper circulation. Moving into the King Library affected the statistics in two fiscal years. However, in the first six months of 2004/2005, the remarkable increase in use of paper government publications appears encouraging. In the first year of the King Library, government publications circulation increased. Surprisingly, in the second year of operation, there is even greater use of government publications. The third set of statistics shows a promising increase of paper copy use in the first six months of the 2004/2005 fiscal year.

The merger of the two libraries increased the importance of tracking government publications use statistics. While the library tracked paper use, tracking electronic use remained out of reach until August 2004. A tracking program developed by the GPO produces a report, "Statistical Reports of PURL Referrals," that answers this need in part. An-

TABLE 1. Government Publications Circulation Statistics

Clark Library Pre-Merged Government Publications Circulation Statistics

Year	Circulation Activity
1982-83	13,098
1986-87	10,928

Clark Library Merged Government Publications Circulation Statistics

Year	Circulation Activity
1999-2000	5,342
2002-2003	1,658*

King Library Merged Government Publications Circulation Statistics

Year	Circulation Activity
2003-2004	1,435**
July 2004-Dec. 2004	912 (6 mos.)

*Low numbers reflect the relocation of government materials to an offsite storage facility during the construction of the new library building.
** August, 2003-June, 2004.

other statistical measure is the use of government publications' web pages. In September 2003, the King Library began to use WebTrends (www.WebTrends.com) to monitor web page usage. These statistics show the seasonal nature of library use (see Table 2).

These statistics for electronic access, along with circulation statistics, help measure and record the level of use of the library as a federal depository. Federal depository libraries are required to serve the community in their region and demonstrate their effectiveness in this effort. The statistics assist in providing a measure of government publications use and benefits of outreach to the public and the university community.

BENEFITS OF MERGED LIBRARIES

First Merger: Clark Library, 1997

The first merger of Government Publications into the Reference Department at SJSU helped identify several major benefits. The role of the professional librarians in designing a workable government publications merger became apparent. The merger fostered the development of leadership and communication skills in reference librarians, reference librarians took a leadership role in designing a professional development program for government publications, and reference librarians became more proficient in using government publications as a result of this program. This professional development program became the model for future programs in the King Library. The Clark Library administra-

TABLE 2. Government Publications Subject Pages Visits

Month	Visits
September-03	200
October-03	390
January-04	201
February-04	109
March-04	443
May-04	499
June-04	189
July-04	136

Note: Statistics are not available for November and December 2003 or for April and August 2004.

tion team acknowledged and supported the ongoing need for professional development programs.

Second Merger: King Library, 2003

The second merger of SJSU and SJPL presented challenges and opportunities on a much larger scale. Whereas the first merger was a one-year process, the planning and the implementation process for the King Library was a seven-year process that continues to this day. Collegial exchanges between the public and academic reference librarians on institutional practices and issues relating to government publications encouraged creative thinking and the development of new practices. In the second merger, reference librarians from both libraries encountered reference questions that provided opportunities to meet the challenges of learning new concepts, teaching diverse communities, and becoming role models for King Library's vision of lifelong learning. In addition, librarians experienced opportunities to grow professionally and gain additional expertise in government publications in this new collaborative setting. Creative and innovative professional development workshops designed by and for librarians filled the need for knowledge of government publications. A sense of collegial participation and ownership emerged which in turn led to professional revitalization. Appendix 2 provides the organizational chart of the merged functions in Reference and Technical Services.

The needs of the new communities of users drove special projects such as the Marcive retrospective project and the importance of the design of the government publications web pages. The addition of the Marcive retrospective records to the online catalog makes the government publications more accessible. The increase in circulation of government publications paper materials is attributed to the Marcive project and the greater size of this new user community. The web pages make government publications more visible to users.

This new merged setting eliminated several barriers to government publications and there is no longer a separate physical department. The size of the collection increased for both the academic and public library community. Access to electronic full-text government documents through the new online catalog system is another barrier eliminated in this merger. The new online catalog system accommodates the needs of both libraries for patron needs and institutional needs. Statistics from 2004 show an increase in use of both paper and electronic government publications. The number of visits to the subject web pages for government publications also continues to increase.

Like the rise in government publications circulation and web page use, requests for presentations increased. The visibility of the King Library results in user groups requesting specialized government publications training. The Library created customized sessions for communities such as university students and faculty, special business community members, members of the general public and professional associations.

CONCLUSION

The Federal Depository Library Program has set standards for performance and accountability. This new King Library with its merged reference service more than meets the required elements of the FDLP in several ways. There is expanded outreach to the community via workshops on subjects of local interest. There is improved access to the publications the Library owns via a retrospective project that is adding bibliographic records from 1986 to the present. Reference service provided by librarians improved through the Library's professional development programs designed to assist in learning the tools and resources of government publications.

Merged reference service is not a static entity. In order to succeed, there must be recognition that not only is the reference merger an ongoing process, but that the access and the resources in government publications in the web environment will require ongoing training sessions. Finally, the merger with reference and, subsequently, the merger between SJSU and SJPL resulted in a tremendous increase in use of library resources. The Reference Services unit in this merger of resources worked hard to embody the vision statement of the King Library to "provide students, instructors and the community access to the information they need for educational and personal growth throughout their lives" (San José Public Libraries and San José State University Library, 2004).

REFERENCES

Aldrich, D., Bertot, J. C., & McClure, C. R. (2002). E-Government: Initiatives, developments, and issues. *Government Information Quarterly, 19*(4), 349-355.

Amata, B. (Ed.). (1996). Shotgun weddings and amicable divorces: Integration vs. separation of government documents and reference services. *DttP: A Quarterly Journal of Government Information Practice and Perspective, 24*(1), 54-66.

City of San José and The Trustees of California State University on behalf of San José State University. (1998). *Agreement for ownership and operation of joint library building and grant of easement* (Memorandum of Understanding). Retrieved August 29, 2004, from http://www.sjlibrary.org/about/locations/king/operating_agreement.pdf.

Farrell, M. P. (2000). Training for documents reference in a merged reference center. *DttP: A Quarterly Journal of Government Information Practice and Perspective, 28*(4), 11-16.

Frazer, S. L., Boone, K. W., & McCart, V. A. (1997). Merging government information and the reference department: A team-based approach. *Journal of Government Information, 24*(2) 93-102.

Hernon, P., & McClure, C. R. (1988). *Public access to government information: Issues, trends, and strategies*. (2nd ed.), Norwood, NJ: Ablex Publishing Corporation.

Kinder, R. (Ed.). (1991). *Government documents and reference services*. New York: The Haworth Press, Inc.

King, V. (2003). Cooperative reference desk scheduling and its effects on professional collegiality. *The Reference Librarian, 83/84,* 97-118.

San José Public Libraries and San José State University Library. (2003). *Early years of San José Public Library, 1849-1970*. Retrieved August 29, 2004, from http://www.sjlibrary.org/about/history/early_sjpl.htm.

San José Public Libraries and San José State University Library. (2004). *Our vision*. Retrieved August 30, 2004, from http://www.sjlibrary.org/about/vision/index.htm.

San José State University. (1997). Academic Priority Steering Committee. *Preliminary academic priorities report*. Unpublished.

San José State University. (1998). *Strategic operational plan for the San José joint library*. Unpublished.

San José State University. (2004). *SJSU history*. Retrieved August 29, 2004, from http://www.sjsu.edu/about_sjsu/history/.

Statistical reports of PURL referrals now available to libraries. (2003). *Administrative Notes, 24*(11), 3. Retrieved January 10, 2005, from http://www.access.gpo.gov/su_docs/fdlp/pubs/adnotes/.

Taylor, S. N., & Schmidt, F. C. (2001). Reference services and federal documents: Current status and issues. *Colorado Libraries, 27*(2), 21-24.

Wilhoit, K. H. (2000). To merge or not to merge–what are the questions? Integrating documents into reference or technical services: Highlights of the GODORT program. *Library Collections, Acquisitions & Technical Services, 24*(2), 310-311.

APPENDIX 1. Joint Library Operational Planning and Roles and Responsibilities

TEAM	MEMBERS	ROLE/RESPONSIBILITIES
Senior Leadership Team	Members: Redevelopment Director, City Manager, University Provost, University Senior VP for Administration, University VP for Advancement, SJPL Library Director, SJSU Dean of Library Services	Provide oversight, coordination, and communication about the Joint Library at the highest administrative levels. Meets quarterly.
SJSU Dean of Library Services; SJPL Library Director		• Lead and direct the operational planning for the Joint Library • Members of Senior Leadership Team • Members of Core Team • Supervise program managers • Assist in fundraising and related activities
Project Managers	SJSU Library Project Manager SJPL Project Manager	• Support and coordinate work of Planning Teams • Provide communication links between the teams • Support Core Team; bring issues forward from planning teams • Establish and maintain timetables, processes, and formats for project activities • Facilitate team meetings and provide training needed • Keep operational planning records and files • Manage consulting contracts • Develop, maintain, and coordinate the operational planning timeline and deliverables; bring issues forward to core Team
Joint Library Program Manager		• Primary liaison for the Joint Library Project to and from all external (not-library) matters relating to the Joint Library • Supervises SJPL Project Manager Position • Member of Core Team, Ex officio
SJPL Supervising Librarian (Main Library) and SJSU Associate Dean		• Assist co-chairs and planning team members in resolving conflicts between day-to-day operational demands and joint library planning activities • Serve as coach and consultant to teams, team members, and co-chairs; attend team meetings as needed

TEAM	MEMBERS	ROLE/RESPONSIBILITIES
Core Team	SJSU and SJPL Project Managers, SJSU Dean of Library Services, SJPL City Librarian, SJPL Supervising Librarian/Main Library, Associate Dean, and SJPL Program Manager	• Review issues brought forward by Program Managers, Project Managers, or Planning Teams and provide advice, obtain information, or make decisions • Establish teams as needed • Review operational planning timeline and activities to ensure effective progress • Provide support to teams and program managers through coordination with outside-the-libraries parties • Provide resources to Planning Teams and Project Managers • Maintain a high level of communication among library managers most responsible for and involved in Joint Library planning
Planning Teams: Co-chairs 1. Policies & Procedures 2. Collection Management & Technical Services 3. Online Systems & Technology 4. User Services 5. Organizational Design & Development 6. Administrative Services	1 SJPL employee 1 SJSU library employee	Lead the work of the team by: • Plan meeting agendas; ensure that agendas are distributed to team members and Project Managers; ensure that meeting notes are recorded, posted, and sent to the Project Managers • Lead and manage team meetings • Track Team workplan/timeline; inform Project Managers of any adjustments needed • Attend co-chair/core team brownbag meetings; attend co-chair meetings • Coordinate with co-chairs of other teams as needed • Encourage positive and active participation of team members in meetings and activities • Identify and attempt to resolve issues that may arise in the team or between the team and other operational planning groups or individuals • Complete evaluation/credit forms for team members
Planning Team Members	SJSU library employees SJPL library employees	• Actively and positively participate in team meetings and activities • Meet deadlines for tasks or activities undertaken as a team member • Complete evaluation/credit forms for co-chairs

APPENDIX 2. Organization and Implementation Plan for Merged Functions in the King Library

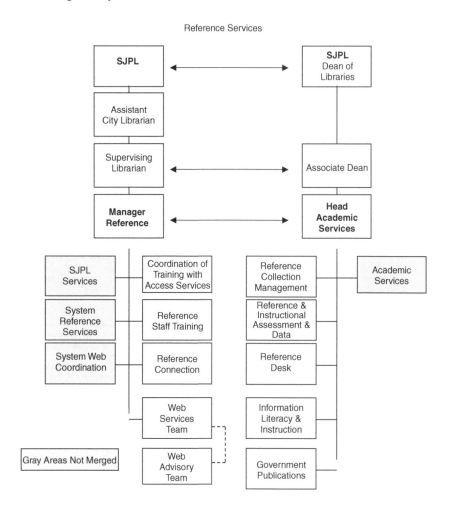

Reference Services

Technical Services

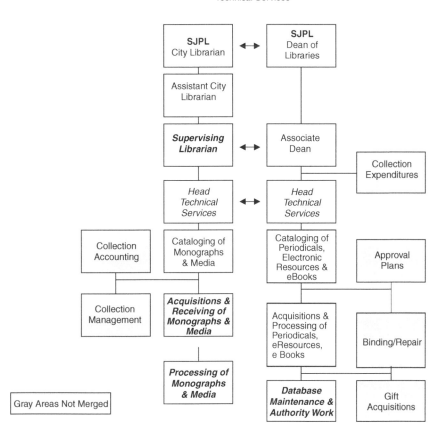

Student Assistant Training
in a Small Academic Library

Ruth Sara Connell
Patricia J. Mileham

SUMMARY. At Valparaiso University's main library, the Christopher Center for Library and Information Resources (formerly the Moellering Library), student employees are an integral part of day-to-day operations. Students work at the reference desk and must be able to handle reference questions. Since the fall 2000 semester, the Reference Services Librarian has been creating a training program for the student assistants, consisting of an initial training period and a series of quizzes combined with review sessions. Student assistants are also indispensable in Instruction Services. These students are charged with library web site and instruction materials' updates. Methods, lessons learned throughout the process, and quiz questions are used to illustrate the development of the training program. Student performance evaluations and feedback are positive. *[Article copies available for a fee from The Haworth Document Delivery Service: 1-800-HAWORTH. E-mail address: <docdelivery@haworthpress.com> Website: <http://www.HaworthPress.com> © 2006 by The Haworth Press, Inc. All rights reserved.]*

Ruth Sara Connell is Reference Services Librarian (E-mail: Ruth.Connell@valpo. edu); and Patricia J. Mileham is Instruction Services Librarian, both at Valparaiso University, Valparaiso, IN 46383.

[Haworth co-indexing entry note]: "Student Assistant Training in a Small Academic Library." Connell, Ruth Sara, and Patricia J. Mileham. Co-published simultaneously in *Public Services Quarterly* (The Haworth Information Press, an imprint of The Haworth Press, Inc.) Vol. 2, No. 2/3, 2006, pp. 69-84; and: *Reference Assessment and Evaluation* (ed: Tom Diamond, and Mark Sanders) The Haworth Information Press, an imprint of The Haworth Press, Inc., 2006, pp. 69-84. Single or multiple copies of this article are available for a fee from The Haworth Document Delivery Service [1-800-HAWORTH, 9:00 a.m. - 5:00 p.m. (EST). E-mail address: docdelivery@haworthpress.com].

KEYWORDS. Reference services, instruction services, student assistants, training program, academic libraries

INTRODUCTION

One Saturday, early in the fall 2000 semester, the Reference Services Librarian at Valparaiso University (VU) came to the library to work on a project. As the head of the Reference Department, the Reference Services Librarian manages reference student assistants and oversees Interlibrary Loan, but also assists in other areas such as instruction and web design. Other librarians work in reference, but they do not report to the Reference Services Librarian. That afternoon, the librarian's supposed fairly short visit turned into a five hour ordeal, largely because the Reference Services Librarian answered reference questions for much of that time. The several student assistants working the reference desk had not been adequately trained to work on their own and kept coming to the librarian for help. This lack of training stemmed from the newness of the reference student assistant program combined with professional turnover in that department. The barrage of questions prompted the Reference Services Librarian to wonder what happened on other Saturdays when she did not come into work. This experience served as the impetus for many changes in the Reference student assistant training program.

LITERATURE REVIEW

There is an extensive selection of books, articles, and web sites focusing upon student training. Several served as benchmarks for this project. David Baldwin's book, *Effective Management of Student Employment: Organizing for Student Employment in Academic Libraries* (2000), is a fundamental resource for any library that employs student assistants. This timely and well-organized book presents both the theoretical and practical aspects of student employment. It serves as a foundational referral tool, as well as guide to good practices.

Two articles in particular helped to put VU's proposed program in context. Edwards' (1990) "Student Staff Training in the Smaller Library" recognizes many of the constraints small libraries work within (such as informality with staff, inconsistency with training, and procedural discontinuity between departments), while also acknowledging the positive aspects of flexibility and adaptability to student needs. While the specific need at VU is student assistant training for reference, instruction, and web work, the Lipow article (1999), " 'In Your Face' Reference Service," is important due to the changing context of reference services and clientele. The author contrasts the passive ways in which librarians traditionally begin patron interaction (e.g., often waiting for the patron to come to a service desk or office) with the new active service models that many patrons are accustomed to in the commercial world: e-mail and chat interactions, roving staff, and online documentation. With examples and suggestions, Lipow encourages libraries to adopt real strategies to meet the needs of a changing clientele.

Many good articles containing pertinent literature reviews and comprehensive reference lists examine various theoretical aspects of student assistant training. Borin's (2001) article offers practical tips and advice while also addressing larger theoretical training issues, such as patrons not making distinctions between librarians and student assistants working at the reference desk and the diversity (or lack thereof) of the student staff. An in-depth model of creating a quality training program is detailed in Kathmans' (2000) article. This article is an essential read for any library beginning a training program or reorganizing an existing one. Its comprehensive nature (i.e., literature review, training problems, a program model, and evaluation of training) provides step-by-step instructions for those creating a new student assistant program as well as serving those struggling with an unsatisfactory program.

While many librarians in instruction and reference consider the various learning styles of students in the classroom context, Burrows' (1995) article is a reminder to consider these differences when training student assistants. She thoughtfully considers some professional librarian issues of student assistant training needs, including over-dependence on a poorly trained workforce due to financial constraints. Constantinou (1998) discusses student assistant motivation in very specific and unique ways, emphasizing that this process should be given the attention and preparation that it deserves. In this way, the student and library supervisor treat one another with professional respect beginning with the initial job interview. While applied to media center student assistants, Beile's (1997) focus of competency-based training (CBT) does a great job of addressing the practical reality of creating a CBT program that is easily adapted to a library situation.

Specific idea and example articles are also very useful when considering program creation or re-design. Based on an ongoing, successful program, Wesley (1990) recounts her library's consideration that the students' meeting with the library director is key, while also encouraging the use of an independent, self-guided, active game (such as well-thought-out scavenger hunt) to serve as an orientation to the library. While every aspect of the University of Northern Iowa's Rod Library student assistant training program is worthy of consideration, author Chris Neuhaus (2001) notes the use of bi-weekly worksheets as both learning and measuring tools has proven highly effective. Even as early as 1985, Guilfoyle advocated the use of computer-assisted training as a rich addition to a program. This excellent article emphasizes that not all training should be done through a computer and then discusses appropriate detail about the planning, design, and benefits such training can provide. Henning's (2000) article specifically addresses a student assistant training program for circulation duties and underscores the fact that an entire library needs to collaborate in the development of a rewarding training program.

A sampling of web sites offers clear examples of what can be done online and with open access to support student assistants. The Houston Cole Library at Jacksonville State University (www.jsu.edu/depart/library/graphic/stuhand.htm) offers a visually clean, easy-to-follow web site designed specifically for its student assistants. Very direct and to-the-point information is available for the students–factual highlights that serve to enhance basic knowledge of their jobs as well as training, hiring, evaluation, and disciplinary procedures. Providing easy access to work forms rewards, and perhaps ensures, students' periodic return to the site. The University of Louisville's University Libraries Student Assistant Training Program (library.louisville.edu/training) web site is enhanced with the inclusion of an "Information for Supervisors" section. Supervisors benefit from a common, consistent resource for student assistant training and evaluation materials. Also following a simple, clean design, the graphics used on this site illustrate many of the procedures the student assistants will learn. This learning is then reinforced with ongoing exercises and the online availability of the entire student assistant handbook. Niederlander's LibrarySupportStaff.com, a site designed to support library paraprofessionals, offers a compilation web page on library student workers. Both print and online resources are recommended, with many links to other student assistant training tools produced by various libraries.

BACKGROUND

Set in northwest Indiana, Valparaiso University is home to 3,600 students, with majors in over 60 fields of study in five colleges (arts & sciences, honors, nursing, engineering, and business). The University also supports a law school with its own library, a graduate division, the College of Adult Scholars, and various other community-focused programs. Moellering Library served as the main library on campus until the fall 2004 semester, when construction of a new building, the Christopher Center for Library and Information Resources, was completed. The main library has over 340,000 print volumes. On staff, there are nine librarians, 13 support staff, and approximately 60 student assistants (per semester). Of those 60, approximately 10 are employed directly each semester by the reference, instruction, and web support departments.

Valparaiso University is a small campus, and while the library is one of the largest student employers on campus, those students available and interested in library reference services work are few. That, in combination with the campus policy that encourages keeping per-student work time to a minimum number of hours per week, keeps the student worker pool shallow. Statistics show a committed student staff after hiring but graduation, internships, and semesters spent studying abroad result in a relatively high turnover.

Likewise, the library staff is small. As department heads, neither the Reference Services Librarian or the Instruction Services Librarian have professional or paraprofessional staff that report directly to them, making it essential to have well-trained, knowledgeable students available to work as close to the start of the semester as possible. Since management of the library web site has always been a part of the Instruction Services Librarian's job, a major portion of time is dedicated to it as well. At VU's main library, there are nine librarians. Two librarians, the Dean of Library Services and the Cataloging Services Librarian, do not work in reference at all. Seven librarians work at the reference desk which is staffed 85 hours a week. Six of the seven (not including the Reference Services Librarian) librarians cover 25 hours a week (mainly evening and Sunday hours). This leaves the Reference Services Librarian with 60 hours a week to cover by herself or with the help of student assistants. Without student help, covering these hours would be impossible. Reference student assistants are a vital and critical necessity at VU.

There is always the issue of the ever-evolving library. Policies change, databases change, and therefore, training is an ongoing project. In addition to revising the training program for each new crop of students, there must be a way to make sure changes reach current student assistants. In order to do this, the Reference Services Librarian used to send e-mails to student assistants announcing each change. However, some students did not read their e-mails or failed to remember the information sent to them. The department needed a better, more accountable system to support growth and change.

Finally, there has long been debate among librarians about the use of students on reference desks. Gabriela Sonntag expressed one of the positive aspects of using students by stating, "It has been shown that students are more likely to discuss their problems with, and feel less intimidated by other students" (Borin, 2001, p. 196). For others, the thought of having paraprofessionals, particularly undergraduate students, on the reference desk is troubling. Theoretically, having a reference librarian at the desk, always available to address and guide students' research questions is ideal; practically, many questions posed by patrons are either quick reference referrals or technology-related. With the quality of patron satisfaction used as a guiding marker, it makes sense for well-trained student assistants to handle the most frequently asked questions, leaving the librarian available for the true research queries. Appropriately making the referral to the librarian demonstrates foundational understanding of true patron service by the student assistants.

REFERENCE SERVICES: OVERVIEW OF CURRENT SITUATION

Over the past four years, the reference assistant training program has constantly evolved. In summer 2000, the Head of the Reference department retired after 16 years. The Reference Services Librarian replaced the Head of Reference and assumed a new title. Until spring 2000, a paraprofessional Reference Assistant worked with the department head and helped with training and supervision of students, but she left the position shortly before the Head of Reference retired. At that time, the Library eliminated the Reference Assistant position.

Other than a few worksheets, very little print material existed concerning student assistant training, largely because the student assistants had not answered reference questions until spring 2000 when the Reference Assistant left the position. The existing worksheets contained ready reference questions such as, "Where are the periodicals?" and "Where would I find *Catch 22* by Joseph Heller?" These questions are good starting points, but do not help train students to answer more complicated reference questions. Students received computer training only through the software program LCEasy, which helps students become familiar with the Library of Congress (LC) call number system necessary for reshelving duties, but not with reference questions. Therefore, the new Reference Services Librarian had to start from scratch upon her arrival. Since she began her new position a week before the start of fall semester in 2000, virtually no training occurred during that first semester. Luckily, the Reference department needed to replace only one of the 10 student assistants employed during the summer. Thus, the lack of an initial training program only adversely affected one student assistant. This situation provided the background when the Saturday afternoon eye-opening experience occurred for the Reference Services Librarian.

During that year, a training program began to develop. The Reference Services Librarian documented or created departmental procedures and instructions for regular student assistants and created a few haphazard quizzes. The second year of training (beginning fall 2001) was much more organized than the first, but still left much to be desired. That semester, four new students needed to be trained. By this time, written procedures and instructions had been created to give students at the beginning of their training, as well as a general outline of training topics to cover. In addition, the students received testing at the end of their training on their retention of topics covered. This test covered important topics such as: how to locate a journal article from a citation, the name of the Dean of Library Services, and the floorplan of the library. Students reacted favorably to this test, saying that the practice proved much more useful than verbal instruction. It required the students to apply all the knowledge demonstrated to them, as well as become familiar with the library web site.

However, there are several major drawbacks to this form of training. First, the training involved a one-time instruction session, and did not continue to test the students' knowledge. For example, when tax season arrived in spring 2001, the Reference Services Librarian sent out an e-mail to all students, explaining how to access tax forms. However, one of the student assistants came to the librarian a week later unable to help a patron who needed the tax forms. When the librarian asked whether the student had read the informational e-mail, the student replied that she had but forgot the content. A continual training and testing program ensures that students who did not retain information are identified, so that the problem can be rectified.

A second problem with the Reference training program is that it lacked a record on the topical training given to each student. Due to the primarily verbal nature of the training, a record did not exist on topics covered in the conversations, but only if the testing covered specific topics. Because of this lack of record, the Reference Services Librarian often asked students whether she covered a particular topic with them. This did not reflect an efficient and organized program. A more reliable accounting system needed to be created. When training one student, it is not hard to remember the topics covered. But with four trainees, a training checklist is needed. Quizzes help account for the topics covered with each student, but a training checklist is now used.

Over the years, student assistants working in VU's main library received training through certain computer programs. For example, every student assistant in both the Reference and Circulation departments uses LCEasy to learn about LC call numbers. However, most reference student training takes place through face-to-face instruction. This instruction consists of discussions about sources and reference tools, as well as direct observation of the Reference Services Librarian as she answers reference questions. Within the Reference department, this training can take days. To some extent, face-to-face training is preferable to computer training, but because it is so time consuming, incorporating more computer and self-learning mechanisms became necessary. Self-guided work has a distinct advantage to in-person training; trainees learn to do work themselves instead of having to absorb knowledge by observation only. For example, one can show a trainee how to locate an article found in a database multiple times, but it probably will not be absorbed until the student performs the task. During the self-guided work, students have the opportunity to ask questions, which helps prevent frustration if they get stuck.

Ultimately, a combination of self-guided paper and computer-based training worked best. Originally, the quizzes were designed to be taken online using our campus courseware system. However, a student who had spent an hour completing the online quiz lost all his answers when he pressed the "back" button on his browser before submitting the quiz. After this unfortunate mistake, we switched to paper quizzes.

The Reference Services Librarian refreshed her skills in designing the quizzes, an unexpected benefit of the process. An expected detriment of creating the quizzes is the time involved. Most of the quizzes have approximately 10 questions and can take an entire morning to create the quiz, locate the answers, and create an answer key. With the student turnover, the questions can be re-used every couple of years. However, due to the continually changing nature of libraries and databases, many questions must be updated each time they are used.

Some university assignments are given every year and quiz questions are created in preparation for those assignments. For example, Valpo Core is the first-year-experience course for all but the honors college freshmen. It encompasses many disciplines including literature, theology, history, philosophy, and the arts. In the second semester of this class, the major paper assignment requires students to select a career, research the issues affecting it, and interview someone in that field. Currently, library instruction is not a requirement for Core, and consequently, only one-fourth of the students receive class time with a librarian and the online course pathfinder. Many of the remaining three-fourths come to the reference desk for help. Anticipating this, extra print copies of the course pathfinders are available at the reference desk; reference student assistants can recommend the online version and they received training and quizzing on the career reference materials. Other quizzes and questions are created in response to actual queries received at the reference desk. Many patrons request literature reviews, so an entire quiz is devoted to the topic in response to these questions.

The reference student assistants are usually given quizzes every month and most have come to enjoy the challenge. Some students score consistently high, while others continue to struggle. This has differentiated the students who need continual guidance from those who are doing well on their own. During late evening shifts and Saturdays, students work without a librarian present. Therefore, it is important that these students working alone have strong reference skills. The quizzes have helped identify strong students, which aids in scheduling.

Some students finish the quizzes in one shift, while others struggle over several days or even a week. There is no time limit and this gives students time to explore the resources available to them. After they finish their quizzes, the Reference Services Librarian takes each student aside and individually reviews the quizzes, comments on things done well, recommends other sources to be considered, and notes questions answered incorrectly. This is time consuming, but an important aid in student learning.

At the end of the fall 2002 semester, several students approached the Reference Services Librarian and asked if they could design their own questions. The students made a challenge out of it. Six out of seven students chose to participate, with each student creating two questions which they submitted to the Reference Services Librarian. She compiled the questions into a quiz and administered it to the students. They decided that the test would be scored based on how many questions they answered correctly, combined with the number of people who answered the questions incorrectly. The students enjoyed this activity and gave their supervisor a break from quiz creation.

Although the Reference department moved to paper quizzes, other reference information was placed online. A print version of policies/procedures would be a waste of paper resources because of frequent changes in the library. The online information manual is easy to update and access throughout the library. It contains the reference student schedule, directions on processing new reference books, shelf-reading, reference closing and opening procedures, student duties, printing policy, directions on using the scanner, and other frequently used procedures and questions. Students commented how much they like the online format.

INFORMATION SERVICES:
OVERVIEW OF THE CURRENT SITUATION

In determining the need for student assistants in the Instruction Services department, which also maintains the vast majority of the library's web site, it is noted that these assistants have almost as much "frontline" importance as those working at Circulation and the Reference desks. Many students are affected by the competence of the library instruction program as well as the library web site, especially those students who access library resources while outside the library. The students who work in these areas not only support the instruction categories of the web site but the site itself.

Instruction is a rapidly growing program within the library. Supported with a team format, it is subject liaison based, which allows user service librarians direct contact with students and teaching faculty. Beginning fall 1999, each library session class has its own web page (pathfinder), tailored to assignments/needs of the class. This is done for a number of useful reasons: teaching multiple sessions of the same class, teaching a class over several days, teaching make-up sessions, and giving the students a comprehensive resource to assist in their assignment completion. Instructors created a total of 92 web-based pathfinders in the 2000-01 academic year, with that number increasing to 111 in the 2002-03 year. While the librarians teaching the class are most often responsible for the content, it is the Instruction Services department that is charged with creating the actual pages themselves.

The Christopher Center for Library and Information Resources web site is another area of rapid growth within the library. At this time, there are approximately 750 active pages, with increases anticipated each semester. Although two other librarians manage specific areas of the site (reference/databases and government information/maps), the bulk of creating and updating the site is the responsibility of the Instruction Services Librarian. Starting in fall 2003, the department supervised a staff intranet site as well.

Instruction Services training presently consists of spending time one-on-one with the students as they work through their first sessions with various duties. Though there is a print manual to guide them with basic questions, this one-on-one time is still very necessary. It also usually coincides with some of the busiest days as students are often hired at the start of semesters. Hopefully, many of the techniques used in Reference Services training will be adaptable to all User Services student assistant training, including those in Instruction Services, Interlibrary Loan, and Circulation.

To assist in User Services, student assistants must have more than just basic interpersonal skills and web coding abilities. Without becoming minors in library science, they must also have some understanding of how libraries work (especially VUs), why things are done in a particular way, and why the library web site is sometimes the most individualized site among the campus' web presence (providing resource access, resource information, general assistance–marks of a very interactive site). They must feel supported in working individually for them to be vested members of the library staff, but yet collegial enough to meet the need of various librarians/instructors, particularly those who are not their direct supervisors.

STUDENT ASSISTANT SURVEY

After the first semester of biweekly quizzes in fall 2002, reference student assistants were polled to see how they felt about the new training program. All students took the survey and 86% agreed or strongly agreed that the quizzes improved their reference skills. When asked to rate their reference skills before training, after the initial training, and at the time they took the survey, 100% said that they felt more confident after the initial training. In addition, 86% felt that their skills improved between the initial training and the time they took the survey. Following are some of their comments.

- "My reference training has greatly impacted my library use as a student. I believe I come to the library more often than I would have if I was not a reference assistant."
- "I definitely know 5 times more about research and what is available than I used to. This has been a great job to have, and very helpful . . . . Every quiz, I learn something new."
- "The quizzes are often much more difficult than any of the reference questions I typically get."
- "It's very hard to learn everything for your job in one or two sittings. It's a job where you're always learning through experiences you have."
- "I was like a fish out of water initially and I felt overwhelmed with all the new information I had to absorb, but I now feel quite at ease helping anyone."

Several students also offered suggestions. Although it is not feasible at this time due to staffing and student schedule issues, one suggested having a monthly training session that all student assistants would attend. Another suggested having new student assistants shadow more experienced students. This idea may be implemented in the future.

FOLLOW-UP:
TRAINING AND ASSESSMENT

At the end of the 2002-03 academic year, reference student assistants took a cumulative quiz. This quiz contained questions from previous quizzes and helped identify how much of the information covered over the year remained with the students. The Reference Services Librarian kept a record of what sources she showed the students when reviewing quizzes, thus a paper trail existed of the material the students *should* have known. The cumulative quiz tested what they *actually* knew. When deciding which questions to include in the quiz, the Reference Services Librarian evaluated questions based on how many students missed those questions, and the reasons for missing the questions. Were the questions missed because they were challenging or because they were poorly worded or designed? The final quiz included challenging, but not confusing, questions used the first time around.

Only five students worked in reference at the time the cumulative quiz was given. One had been hired mid-year and therefore had only taken half the monthly quizzes. The new student picked things up quickly and did well, but she still scored several points lower (5 out of a possible 11 points) than any of the more experienced student assistants. Most of the questions she missed were harvested from quizzes she had not taken. The students who had taken all the quizzes did fairly well, most getting 8 or 9 correct out of 11.

Although the pool of students was small, the results of this final cumulative quiz help illustrate how useful the quizzes are in teaching students research sources and skills. This combination of ongoing assessment, student feedback, and librarian response should help to ensure that the training needs of our students are met while meeting the assistance needs of our patrons.

Unfortunately, only one student worked continuously from fall 2002 through spring 2004. No students quit their jobs, but due to students leaving and returning from study abroad experiences, student teaching, and attrition through graduation, the library encountered almost 100% turnover over two years. Newly hired students started the quizzes from the beginning, and students returning from study abroad took quizzes assigned in their absences. One new quiz style emerged in the 2003-04 academic year. Instead of having students complete a series of questions, they might have to do some research on a particular topic. For example, in one quiz they had to find literary criticisms for Margaret Atwood's *The Handmaid's Tale*. Due to the high turnover, it is difficult to see the long-term effect of the training program.

CONCLUSION

An abundance of information to cover made it hard to know where to begin when developing this training program. While it is true that there is a plethora of knowledge required to effectively serve at the reference desk, topics can be addressed individually in the quizzes by dividing them into subtopics that are much more manageable in depth and breadth.

With extensive training, student assistants can effectively answer the majority of questions received at the reference desk. Training is an ongoing process, not a one-shot session when students are initially hired. Spreading training material out throughout the year allows students time to reflect on what they have learned, which encourages retention of knowledge more than an initial training period would. The training also appears to empower the student assistants so that they are more confident answering questions. One student assistant recently commented that he could see how an aspect of the research process would be difficult for the uninitiated, but that is easy for "those of *us* in the (library) field"!

Here are some questions and possible topics for future research that arose from this project.

* Are student patrons more comfortable approaching their peers (fellow students) or would they prefer to work with librarians? Do they know the difference?
* How do teaching faculty feel about asking questions of students on the reference desk?
* Is patron satisfaction affected when questions are answered by student assistants rather than librarians?
* How effective would it be to cross-train student assistants for different User Service departments (Reference, Instruction, Government Documents, Periodicals, and Circulation)?

The purpose of designing an effective training program for our students is that patrons will be better served. With training, student assistants can answer the everyday research questions, and librarians can spend more time focusing on the patrons with complicated research queries, in addition to having more time to do other projects that will improve service for end-users.

REFERENCES

Baldwin, D. A., Wilkinson, F. C., & Barkely, D. C. (2000). *Effective management of student employment: Organizing for student employment in academic libraries.* Englewood, CO: Libraries Unlimited.

Beile, P. M. (1997). Great expectations: Competency-based training for student media center assistants. *MC Journal: The Journal of Academic Media Librarianship, 5*(2). Retrieved August 31, 2004, from http://wings.buffalo.edu/publications/mcjrnl/v5n2/beile.html.

Borin, J. (2001). Training, supervising, and evaluating student information assistants. *The Reference Librarian, 72,* 195-206.

Burrows, J. H. (1995). Training student workers in academic libraries: How and why? *The Journal of Library Administration, 21*(3/4), 77-86.

Constantinou, C. (1998). Recruiting, training, and motivating student assistants in academic libraries. *Catholic Library World, 69*(2), 20-23.

Edwards, R. A. (1990). Student staff training in the smaller library. *The Journal of Library Administration, 12*(2), 89-95.

Guilfoyle, M. C. (1985). Computer-assisted training for student library assistants. *The Journal of Academic Librarianship, 10*(6), 333-336.

Henning, M. M. (2000). Expanding the role of the student desk assistant in the electronic environment. *College & Undergraduate Libraries, 7*(1), 11-24.

Houston Cole Library. *Student assistant handbook.* (n.d.). Retrieved August 31, 2004, from Jacksonville State University, http://www.jsu.edu/depart/library/graphic/stuhand.htm.

Kathman, J. M., & Kathman, M. D. (2000). Training student employees for quality service. *The Journal of Academic Librarianship, 26*(3), 176-182.

Lipow, A. G. (1999). 'In your face' reference service. *Library Journal, 124*(13), 50-52.

Neuhaus, C. (2001). Flexibility and feedback: A new approach to ongoing training for reference student assistants. *Reference Services Review, 29*(1), 53-64.

Niederlander, M. (n.d.). *Library student workers.* In LibrarySupportStaff.com: Resources for on the job in libraries. Retrieved February 14, 2005, from http://www.librarysupportstaff.com/students4libs.html.

University of Louisville Libraries. *Student assistant training program.* (n.d.). Retrieved August 30, 2004, from University of Louisville Libraries, http://library.louisville.edu/training.

Wesley, T. L. (1990). Beyond job training: An orientation program for library student assistants. *Catholic Library World, 61*(5), 215-217.

APPENDIX

SAMPLE QUIZ QUESTIONS

1. Describe, in a few sentences, the difference between primary and secondary sources.

2. What were Procter & Gamble's net sales for the past five fiscal years? Where did you find this information?

3. Someone calls and says they are trying to access the Chronicle of Higher Education online, so they need the password. What is the password, and can you give it out to them?

4. What is the title and who wrote the poem that ends "Though but a cat lies buried here."

5. Find citations for two reviews of Barbara Kingsolver's book "Prodigal Summer." Write citation information here.

6. What is the name of the company that owns KFC? Source?

7. A patron comes in looking for the text of Title 27, chapter two of the U.S. Code. What are the subjects of the title and chapter?

8. The U.S. Code is published every 6 years. During the interim period, supplements are produced with updated laws. The government is currently producing the 2000 edition. We have received most of the updated 2000 edition, but not all. When the 2000 edition of Title 50 arrives, which 1994 volumes can be withdrawn? List them here.

9. Do we have this article here? If so, where? If not, what should you tell the patron?

   Effects of Normal Aging and Alzheimer's Disease on Emotional Memory. By: Kensinger, Elizabeth A.; Brierley, Barbara; Medford, Nick; Growdon, John H.; Corkin, Suzanne; Source: Emotion. Vol. 2 (2) June 2002, pp. 118-134.

10. I want to do a database search for bibliographic instruction (BI) in colleges and high schools (that is, I want articles on BI that relate to either high school or college). Which of the following is the correct Boolean combination?

    a. bibliographic instruction OR (college students AND high school students)

    b. bibliographic instruction AND (college students OR high school students)

    c. bibliographic instruction AND (college students AND high school students)

Comparing Virtual Reference Exit Survey Results and Transcript Analysis: A Model for Service Evaluation

Joanne B. Smyth
James C. MacKenzie

SUMMARY. This study uses virtual reference transcripts for which patrons completed exit surveys to seek any correlations between user and librarian satisfaction within virtual reference transactions. By analyzing transcripts with a focus on three elements–technology performance, preferred reference practices, and the demonstrated communication levels of both the library staff member and the patron–the authors sought to determine whether these three elements had any bearing on satisfaction in virtual reference sessions. *[Article copies available for a fee from The Haworth Document Delivery Service: 1-800-HAWORTH. E-mail address: <docdelivery@haworthpress.com> Website: <http://www.HaworthPress.com> © 2006 by The Haworth Press, Inc. All rights reserved.]*

KEYWORDS. Academic libraries, exit surveys, librarian satisfaction, reference services, user surveys, virtual reference

Joanne B. Smyth is Coordinator for Distance Education and LIVE Online Reference Service (E-mail: jsmyth@unb.ca); and James C. MacKenzie is Information Services Librarian (E-mail: jmackenz@unb.ca), both at the Harriet Irving Library, University of New Brunswick (Fredericton) Libraries, Fredericton, New Brunswick, Canada, E3B 5H5.

[Haworth co-indexing entry note]: "Comparing Virtual Reference Exit Survey Results and Transcript Analysis: A Model for Service Evaluation." Smyth, Joanne B., and James C. MacKenzie. Co-published simultaneously in *Public Services Quarterly* (The Haworth Information Press, an imprint of The Haworth Press, Inc.) Vol. 2, No. 2/3, 2006, pp. 85-105; and: *Reference Assessment and Evaluation* (ed: Tom Diamond, and Mark Sanders) The Haworth Information Press, an imprint of The Haworth Press, Inc., 2006, pp. 85-105. Single or multiple copies of this article are available for a fee from The Haworth Document Delivery Service [1-800-HAWORTH, 9:00 a.m. - 5:00 p.m. (EST). E-mail address: docdelivery@haworthpress.com].

Available online at http://www.haworthpress.com/web/PSQ
© 2006 by The Haworth Press, Inc. All rights reserved.
doi:10.1300/J295v02n02_07

INTRODUCTION

For almost as long as libraries have provided reference services, they have attempted to evaluate the range and quality of this service, using various approaches and including such diverse elements as the strength of the collection (Lancaster, 1984), the nature of the question (Sears, 2001), demographic information about the user (Lancaster, 1984), and even the environment in which the question is posed (Aluri, 1993). Some examine user satisfaction at the close of the session, or later, while others rely on the library staff members' assessment of the process to identify strengths and weaknesses. Bunge and Murfin's Wisconsin-Ohio Reference Evaluation Program (Bunge, 1999) is an attempt to bring the two perspectives together in a coherent manner.

Reference evaluation has been hampered by concerns regarding user privacy, staff members' professional autonomy, and the obtrusiveness of any evaluation method employed. However, since the introduction of virtual, real-time reference service, it is possible to approach an evaluation of how we serve our users while preserving user and librarian/staff anonymity and without interfering in the reference process itself. By analyzing transcripts of virtual reference sessions and comparing them with completed user exit surveys, we can gauge satisfaction with the service and learn if and when our success intersects with user satisfaction. This study looks for evidence of a correlation between librarian and user satisfaction with virtual reference transactions, the bases of this satisfaction, and how the divergent values of libraries and their users might contribute to any differences.

LITERATURE REVIEW

Virtual reference first appeared in the form of e-mail correspondence between libraries and their users in the mid-1980s. Since that time, researchers have been trying to apply traditional reference service assessment practices to these exchanges. For the most part, these reports have been one of two types: those dealing with reference processes and those attempting to assess the actual content of the exchanges.

Process studies are typified by Young and Sears' work in gathering statistics to describe the numbers of questions posed in this new medium and the time spent answering them, the types of questions asked (Sears, 2001; Carter & Janes, 2000), and demographic information regarding the users (Young, 1984; Sears, 2001). Perhaps impressed by the popularity of this new communication medium, these studies seem preoccupied with accounting for virtual reference, to identify its place as a service venue within traditional libraries.

Content-oriented studies provide a broader view of virtual reference services, and examine such aspects as librarians' job satisfaction and demonstrated behaviors (Janes, 2002; Lancaster, 1984; Adams & Judd, 1984) in providing these services. Marsteller and Mizzy (2003) have examined the quality of virtual reference interactions, with Lancaster (1984) focusing on whether the question was answered. Others have attempted to scrutinize factors that are outside the librarian's control, to see how these influence success or failure in reference services (Aluri, 1993; Murfin, 1995; Lancaster, 1984).

Not all content-oriented studies have restricted themselves to the librarian's or institution's perspective. Durrance (1995) studies users' "willingness to return" to a specific library staff member as an indicator of service success. Dewdney and Ross (1994) attempt to describe users' experiences in consulting Reference staff. However, there is considerable debate about the reliability of users' stated opinions; to some they are unreliable (Bunge, 1999; Whitlatch, 2001; Richardson, 2002), but others consider them the best source for evaluation (Murfin, 1995).

These studies are hampered by the need to remain unobtrusive while observing reference exchanges. They also fail to consider closely the effects of both the librarian and user's communication levels, in situations where clear communication is essential. Online chat involves the use of written communication; chatters cannot make use of body language, facial expressions, or tone of voice. They must manage to convey their messages textually, but frequently fail to do so. When written communication is weak, a virtual reference session is hampered. This study is able to incorporate both unobtrusive observation and an analysis of both parties' communication levels by examining the transcripts of actual virtual reference sessions conducted in real-time and with the availability of co-browsing library resources.

DESIGN AND METHODOLOGY

Sampling

This study is an attempt to identify correlations between users' and library staff members' reports of virtual reference service success and failure. Exit surveys completed by users completing virtual reference sessions with library staff using LIVE (Library Information in a Virtual Environment), the University of New Brunswick (UNB) Libraries' virtual reference service, provided the originating data.

LIVE is offered to all members of the University of New Brunswick and Saint Thomas University's (STU) academic communities, in Fredericton, New Brunswick, Canada. This includes distance education and other off-campus students, which make up approximately 27% of LIVE use. This study makes use of transcripts generated between mid-September 2002 and mid-February 2003, for which users completed exit surveys at the close of the session. There are a total of 58 transcripts in this grouping, taken from a total set of 223 for the time period, providing us with a sample representing 26% of the total calls to LIVE for the period. These individuals are, for the most part, undergraduate students from UNB or STU. It is important to bear in mind that this exit survey is heavily patron-reaction oriented (Bunge, 1999). Only those who feel strongly enough about the service responded.

Data Collection

The data collection for this study comes from two sources, and uses both quantitative and qualitative methods. The first source is the users' responses to questions in the exit survey (see Appendix 1) on which they are asked for brief information about their status, use of LIVE in the past, and to complete four statements related to their level of satisfaction with the service. The survey concludes with an opportunity for users to volunteer to take part in more in-depth evaluation in the future and with an open comments field.

This study employed the survey because it is the only way to elicit the opinions of LIVE users while the details of the session, its utility, and relevance are still fresh in their minds. The questionnaire method serves as a means of uniform data collection for comparison purposes. Results from this survey are compiled at Tutor.com, formerly LSSI, from whom UNB Libraries purchased a "seat" that enables our library system to monitor calls made by our patrons to their remotely-hosted conferencing site with their virtual reference software, and sent as .csv files to our office, with each session labeled by its call identification number.

The second data source is assembled by analyzing the actual call transcripts for sessions for which exit surveys are completed. These are stripped of any identifying information (names, e-mail IDs, phone numbers, references to courses or instructors, etc.) by a member of our staff who does not perform the analysis. The transcripts are rated by other members of the Reference department staff, both librarians and para-professionals. Their analysis is performed using specific criteria developed by members of the Reference department, using 13 questions that are explained in greater detail in Appendix 2. These questions are intended to address three themes in the transaction process:

1. Technology
2. Reference practices
3. Communication Levels

The questions are presented in Appendix 2, along with values for possible answers, but are listed briefly here:

Technology:

1. What level of connection was made?
2. What was the session duration?
3. How was the session ended?

Reference practices:

4. Was a reference interview conducted?
5. Was the question factual or sources in nature?
6. If the question was sources in nature, did the library staff member take the caller to the required resource, or simply give directions to it?
7. Which tier, as described in the Harriet Irving Library's Tiered Reference service model, does this question address?
8. Given the service expectations at this tiered reference level, was the question completely and accurately answered?

Communications levels:

9. What level of written communication did the caller demonstrate?
10. What level of written communication did the library staff member demonstrate?
11. Overall, what is the level of communication between the two parties?

General:

12. Was an expression of thanks made by the caller during the session?
13. What is your overall assessment of this session? How do you think both parties felt at its close? Factor in the quality of information provided.

We chose to focus on technology, reference practices, and communication levels because they are areas that our department identified as concerns within virtual reference. Technology has a huge impact on the success or failure of any virtual reference session. We are employing software that is still in development and experienced technological disruptions in LIVE throughout its existence. Bandwidth, server traffic, incompatibilities with Macs and Netscape browsers, and unexplained failures dot the landscape of virtual reference. One cannot discuss the levels of success in virtual reference without considering the limitations of this venue.

Our questions dealing with reference practice are part of an assessment of how well the activities associated with good reference service in a traditional setting (Tyckoson, 2001) are carried through to the online environment. Our staff feared the abandonment of negotiating reference interviews, given the expectations for speed in most online communication. Similarly, some felt the erosion in the instructional role of our reference service, with staff instead providing speedy answers online, or giving scant instructions so that they can move on to the next call in the queue.

Communication questions are perhaps the most interesting. Much has been written about the altered communication style evident in online environments. Crystal (2001) describes in detail the truncated, hybrid language that is Netspeak, and its "overlapping mode" that creates a verbal leapfrog game in most transcripts. Yet, written communication is all that our staff and users have to express themselves in LIVE. Within weeks of launching our online service, we received many questions from staff regarding how to understand users' poor writing techniques, whether to join in and adopt their cyber-style, and how to coax meaningful input from callers regarding their information needs. While we were fairly confident of our staff members' writing abilities, we felt that both parties' skills should be addressed. Finally, because in online communication there are times when two competent communicators fail to make their meanings clear to each other, we looked at the overall level of communication evident in the session.

Method

LIVE, introduced in September 2001, uses Tutor.com's virtual reference software and enables librarians and callers to co-browse online resources and access a transcript of their chat session, including the URLs of all links visited, at the end of each session. The staff members who answer calls to LIVE are part of UNB's Harriet Irving Library Reference department, who use a team approach to providing tiered reference services to library users at a centralized information desk. A designated personal computer is located near the information desk to receive calls from virtual reference patrons. Queries can be made in-person, by phone, or through LIVE, our virtual reference service.

For every online exit survey returned to our library by a user during the time frame of the study, we pulled the corresponding transcript, stripped of identifying information, and evaluated using the 13-item question list as noted in Appendix 2. Spreadsheet software (Microsoft Excel) is used to record values for each question on each transcript. Totals for each theme are tallied and recorded, along with overall scores. Higher scores (out of a possible total of 37 points) indicate greater levels of success from the library staff perspective, while lower scores indicate less desirable sessions.

Similarly, we integrated the users' exit surveys (Appendix 1) into the spreadsheet program. Null values are assigned to the responses to demographic questions and volunteering to take part in further assessment. For question 3, responses to the four questions are ranked in value from 1-5 and correspond to the Likert scale of users' satisfaction for a total of 20 possible points.

Data Analysis

Data comparison occurred in a number of ways, using the following breakdowns:

1. Top ten in ranking, according to librarian assessment.
2. Bottom ten in ranking, according to librarian assessment.
3. Top ten in ranking, according to user assessment.
4. Bottom ten in ranking, according to user assessment.

5. Proportion of sessions in which both library and user rank session as satisfactory.
6. Proportion of sessions in which both library and user rank session as unsatisfactory.
7. Proportion of sessions rated highly or poorly by users, and in which communication level is high/low.
8. Proportion of sessions rated highly or poorly by users, and in which technology failed or worked well.
9. Proportion of sessions rated highly or poorly by users, and in which the completeness and accuracy of service provided were rated as high/low.
10. User comments from the open comment field, for the top and bottom ten according to the librarians' assessment.

EXPECTED RESULTS

Overall, we expected to find the librarians' assessments of the transcripts to be more stringent than the users'. The librarians' assessments are done after the fact and by the application of predetermined criteria listed in Appendix 2, whereas the users' assessments in Appendix 1 are completed immediately following each session, and convey their cognitive and affective responses to the service received. Our experience with LIVE has shown it to be very popular with users, who provide very few negative comments in their exit surveys. On the other hand, our library staff members tend to temper their enthusiasm for virtual reference with concern for reference practices. They are generally satisfied with the quality of reference service through LIVE.

We anticipated greater correlations between library staff member and user assessments of sessions in which the satisfaction levels are high, and a reduced rate of correlation for sessions in which library staff member satisfaction levels are low, because of the disparate approaches to evaluation. It seemed likely that sessions in which communication levels are high would be evaluated well by both the library staff members and the users, as these tend to be sessions in which both parties contribute meaningfully to the virtual reference transaction. Poor communication invariably leads to frustration for both, so we anticipated low user ratings for these sessions. Similarly, sessions in which the technology failed to enable complete use of the system, or terminated sessions entirely are likely to be rated poorly by our users, as by our library staff.

We find that users often misinterpret system failures as library staff members' deliberate termination of the session.

Users' open comments would perchance provide the most illuminating insight into their perspectives regarding our virtual reference service, revealing some of the elements of reference service that are valuable to users. Judging from exit surveys viewed to date, the bases for user satisfaction involve convenience, ease of use, novelty of online communication, and the chance to have a one-on-one session with library staff. Since 27% of LIVE users are off-campus students, the opportunity to communicate directly with library staff is especially valued. We did not expect to find comments that explicitly place value upon technology, reference practices, or communication levels, as these are elements whose merit is determined by the culture and ambitions, the social norms of the library. Instead, we expected to be able to begin defining what aspects of online reference service are important to users and what may be lacking in sessions that the library staff deems satisfactory but the user does not.

RESULTS

Overall Satisfaction

Although 58 patron surveys and corresponding transcripts are available, in eight cases the transcript indicated a completely failed connection or disconnect that occurred before any interaction between patron and librarian could take place. Since no transcript analysis is possible, those sessions are excluded from the final analysis.

Since the patron survey questionnaire and our own assessment questions are completely different, direct question-by-question comparisons are impossible. To facilitate a comparison of overall satisfaction, a score is calculated for each session as a total of points in each session divided by the total number of possible points, both for the patron and the librarian, resulting in a percentage value. For example, the 13 questions used for the librarians' transcript evaluations (Appendix 2) provide a total of 37 possible points. If the librarian's evaluation resulted in 32 points, a "satisfaction score" of 86.4% would be achieved. A patron exit survey receiving 13 of a possible 20 points resulted in a satisfaction score of 65%. Questions which might not serve as an indicator of a better or worse session (as in session time, for instance) are omitted from this calculation. Across all sessions, average patron satisfaction scored 86.7%, substantially higher than the library's average assessment of 74.2%. Beyond the comparison of librarian and patron satisfaction levels, this overall satisfaction score is also used to gauge patrons' overall satisfaction levels in relation to the three themes of the transaction process (technology, reference practices, and communication levels).

Overall, the analysis is somewhat clouded by positive patron exit survey responses and resulting satisfaction scores. In attempting to identify the 10 highest ranked patron surveys, 15 surveys are found to have "perfect" scores (100% satisfaction). On the library side, the 10 highest ranked assessments ranged from 86% to 97% satisfaction. Interestingly, relatively little overlap occurred between the two lists; only 3 of the 15 "perfect" patron survey sessions also appeared on our own top ten. Similarly, in the lists of 10 lowest-ranked sessions, patron responses coincided with only two of our own. Here, patron responses ranged from 40% to 80% (only one response dipped below 60%), in comparison with librarian assessments from 46% to 62%.

Patron comments associated with transcripts in our own top and bottom ten assessments are also examined. With our own top ten list, eight patrons left comments, seven of which are positive. They ranged from a simple thanks to the very flattering:

- "Staff member was very helpful, and eager to help me with my questions."
- ". . . fantastic service and germane results."
- "Comes in handy when you're in a bind and have something due the next morning."
- "I consider myself to be quite competent. . . but even we have problems with certain things."

At the bottom ten, we received five patron comments; two are brief but positive, two are somewhat neutral ("didn't get my question answered, but did get sent to a location that hopefully can answer it") and the last simply noted "[this] takes too long." It is worth noting that none of the comments, save for the one about being in a bind, explicitly mentions the technological novelty or remote availability as we might have expected. Expressions of satisfaction (or lack of) reflect upon service received rather than the medium of delivery.

Question 13 (Appendix 2), the final transcript analysis question, provided us with another means of comparing overall patron and librarian satisfaction, where we rated the session on a scale of 1-4. We identified

30 sessions that we rated as either "satisfactory" or "highly satisfactory." We then looked to the patron exit surveys, to find those that ranked as satisfactory or higher (where the tally totaled 12 or better from a possible 20), and found that in each case where we had ranked the session as satisfactory, patrons are in agreement. We were less in agreement on what constitutes a marginal or unsatisfactory session. However, we assigned lower overall assessments to 20 sessions, as opposed to only 6 patron exit survey sessions which totaled 11 points or less, agreeing in only 4 cases.

Satisfaction scores for patrons and librarians are also compared for each individual session. Librarians' and patrons' satisfaction scores are within +/−15% in 24 of 50 sessions. Where the gap between the two is 16% or more, patrons' satisfaction scores are almost always higher (24 of 26 sessions). The remaining two sessions displayed a difference where patron evaluations are substantially lower than ours. In one case, our assessment was also relatively low, though not within the +/− 15% margin. In the remaining case, we had actually rated the session quite highly, but the patron's survey response is lukewarm, with a very poor rating in the "hours" question, and the comment attached to the survey made clear that the patron, in spite of what appeared to us to be a good session, left frustrated: "I don't like going to the library and I hate it even more when I use [the catalogue] or search for journals. It never works for me. . . " Although not all lower-scored sessions are accompanied by a comment, this incident provides a reminder that good evaluations (in this case, our own) may not tell the whole story.

Impact of Transaction Elements

Our evaluation of technology performance is based on our assessment of "connection level," with 5 possible levels, ranging from no connection to interact with full co-browsing (question 1, Appendix 2). Where no connection occurred, we are obviously unable to make an assessment of the session (nothing happened), and we eliminated these eight sessions from the final analysis. However, remember that the original 58 sessions were identified because the patron had filled out the survey; eight people are unable to connect or terminated too quickly to make an assessment, but went ahead and filled out the survey anyway. The scores for those eight people ranged from 30% (understandably) to 100%! Forty of the 50 remaining cases employed co-browsing to some extent, and in 30 of those cases there are no failures (all databases worked properly within the software, no discernable technical problems). The range of satisfaction scores moves from a low of 40%, all the way up to 100%. We are unable, then, to find any clear relationship between the software working well or very well and high ratings of patron satisfaction. The remaining 10 cases proved inconclusive for connection level. In these cases, not enough information is available in the transcript to determine whether or not a technology failure occurred, but it did not appear as though co-browsing had been engaged or required. In nine out of the 10 cases, the patron reported a satisfaction level of 80% or better.

In the "reference practices" section of the evaluation (Appendix 2), question 8 measured the "completeness and accuracy" of the librarian's help or answer with a value ranking from 1-3. Our analysis grouped the sessions according to these values and average "satisfaction" values are calculated for each group. Here, we found that, regardless of our assessment of the completeness and accuracy, the patron satisfaction average varied very little, remaining between 85% and 90% whether the answer is judged accurate or inaccurate. The librarians' overall satisfaction scores varied much more, averaging from 79% for the sessions judged to have been answered completely and accurately, to a low of 65.7% for those judged to be incomplete and inaccurate. In virtual reference, as in face-to-face reference, our patrons are often not in the best position to judge our accuracy. Not surprisingly, our assessment of completeness and accuracy does not appear to be closely related to patrons' overall satisfaction with these sessions.

With our analysis of communication levels, we found that our own satisfaction seems quite closely related to communication; as our assessment of the quality of communication (whether the librarians' or the patrons' or overall) increases, so does our satisfaction with the overall session. No clear relationship between average patron satisfaction and the quality of communication emerged. In our evaluations, we judged the librarians to be communicating adequately 88% of the time and patrons about 72% of the time.

Significance

In order to decrease the distance between library staff and user values in reference service, especially within a user-centered paradigm, we must first identify instances in which the two are not in accord. If a session has fulfilled the requirements for success from the library staff's perspective, why might that same session displease a user? We are obliged to reassess these instances where library staff values do not satisfy the relevance or utility criteria of our users, finding ways to integrate the aims and needs of both parties. This evokes a paradox of contradictory values, when libraries' ideas regarding sound research and service practices are somehow incongruent with their users' expectations.

Perhaps most baffling are situations in which library staff members' assessments of sessions are negative, but patrons nevertheless express satisfaction with the event. This coincidence may be a sort of "Hawthorn effect," in which their generosity is attributable to users' enthusiasm for the new medium of virtual reference, and not to the content of the transaction that took place there. As Bunge states, ". . . because patrons appreciate any attention and help they receive, they will report satisfaction even when the information they receive is less than completely useful" (Bunge, 1999, p. 117). The reasons for patron satisfaction in these cases, once identified, can inform future reference policy. We must ask if libraries can do more to provide personal contact with their users, or offer services beyond normal operating hours. Reference departments especially should be looking for ways to expand their presence within online environments, and must include user values in their planning.

CONCLUSION

This study uses qualitative and quantitative data gathered from exit survey questionnaires and an analysis of transcripts from UNB Libraries' virtual reference service to determine if and when user satisfaction with the service provided correlates with library staff satisfaction regarding the transaction. The study uses a selection of transcripts from sessions that took place between September, 2002 and February, 2003, for which users completed exit surveys at the end of the session. This sample includes 25% of the total calls made to LIVE during that period. Patrons' responses on the exit survey are compared with library staff members' assessments of the corresponding transcript, which pay particular attention to technology, reference practices, and communication levels. The primary goal of this study is to identify correlations and non-correlations between satisfaction levels in the two, and to begin identifying the values associated with user satisfaction and dissatisfaction.

In the present study, patron surveys indicated high levels of satisfaction with virtual reference services. While we may take comfort in that fact, this overwhelmingly positive response has proven problematic in our attempts to more clearly distinguish the reasons for that satisfaction, or to note problem areas in need of attention. It is difficult to align patron satisfaction or dissatisfaction with respect to any one of the transaction themes identified by reference staff. More often, overall satisfaction varies independently of technology performance, the library's assessment of completeness and accuracy, and effective communication.

In evaluating session transcripts, library staff members were able to identify a number of sessions where the transaction was deemed unsatisfactory or only marginally satisfactory. In spite of this, patron responses still tended to be very positive. Within the study sample, only on a single occasion was patron satisfaction very low in contrast with a high rating from the library. Certainly we can surmise that the immediacy factor of getting service when and where it is needed may be the most decisive element of service, though few comments stated so explicitly. However, these discrepancies may suggest that the transaction themes that we have identified as most significant somehow miss the mark in identifying what may be of most value to patrons in virtual reference services. This study may spawn further research, including focus groups with the users who volunteered to take part in further evaluation in the exit surveys. These focus groups may identify in greater detail the values of our users. This study can also be repeated at other academic institutions that use virtual reference, and the results can be compared and contrasted.

It will be interesting to reassess user exit surveys and transcript analysis in a longitudinal study. At present, the medium of virtual reference is new and enjoys the spotlight as an innovation in service for library users. Users are still enthusiastic about the medium, and may be overly generous in their appraisal of service received there. Library staff members, while supportive of virtual reference, are concerned about how the medium may change reference service, and challenge its precepts. Once virtual reference is as familiar to both as telephone service, we may revisit this study.

REFERENCES

Adams, M., & Judd, B. (1984). Evaluating reference librarians: Using goal analysis as a first step. *The Reference Librarian*, 11, 131-145.

Aluri, R. (1993). Improving reference service: The case for using a continuous quality improvement method. *RQ*, *33*(2), 220-236.

Bunge, C. A. (1999). Gathering and using patron and librarian perceptions of question-answering success. *The Reference Librarian*, 66, 115-141.

Carter, J., & Janes, J. (2000). Unobtrusive data analysis of digital reference questions and service at the Internet Public Library: An exploratory study. *Library Trends*, *49*(2), 251-265.

Crystal, D. (2001). *Language and the Internet.* Cambridge: Cambridge University Press.

Dewdney, P., & Ross, C. S. (1994). Flying a light aircraft: Reference service evaluation from a user's viewpoint. *RQ*, *34*(2), 217-230.

Durrance, J. (1995). Factors that influence reference success: What makes questioners willing to return? *The Reference Librarian*, 49/50, 243-265.

Janes, J. (2002). Digital reference: Reference librarians' experiences and attitudes. *Journal of the American Society for Information Science and Technology*, *53*(7), 549-566.

Lancaster, F. W. (1984). Factors influencing the effectiveness of question-answering services in libraries. *Reference Librarian*, 11, 95-108.

Marsteller, M. R., & Mizzy, D. (2003). Exploring the synchronous digital reference interaction for query types, question negotiation, and patron response. *Internet Reference Services Quarterly*, *8*(1/2), 149-166.

Murfin, M. E. (1995). Evaluation of reference service by user report of success. *The Reference Librarian*, 49/50, 229-242.

Richardson, Jr., J. V. (2002). Reference is better than we thought. *Library Journal*, *127*(7), 41-42.

Sears, J. (2001, Fall). Chat reference service: An analysis of one semester's data. *Issues In Science and Technology Librarianship*, *32*, article 2. Retrieved November 20, 2004, from http://www.istl.org/01-fall/article2.html.

Tyckoson, D. A. (2001). What is the best model of reference service? *Library Trends*, *50*(2), 183-196.

Whitlatch, J. B. (2001). Evaluating reference services in the electronic age. *Library Trends*, *50*(2), 207-218.

Young, W. F. (1984). Evaluating the reference librarian. *The Reference Librarian*, 11, 123-129.

APPENDIX 1. LIVE Exit Survey

LIVE Exit Survey

The LIVE online reference service is in its trial phase. Your input is essential to us in assessing the usefulness of this service, and in finding ways to improve it. Please take a moment to complete the brief survey below. Thank-you.

1. I am a(n):

    ○ graduate

    ○ undergraduate

    ○ faculty

    ○ other [_____]

2. I have used LIVE in the past.

    ○ Yes

    ○ No

3. Please rate the following:

	Strongly Agree	Agree	Neutral	Disagree	Strongly Disgree
Based on my experience using LIVE today, I will use the service again.	○	○	○	○	○
This LIVE session made me aware of different kinds of information sources.	○	○	○	○	○
The existing service hours for LIVE suit my needs.	○	○	○	○	○
An online reference service such as LIVE should continue to be offered by the library.	○	○	○	○	○

4. I would be willing to take part in a more in-depth evaluation of this service:

    ○ Yes, my e-mail address is [_____]

    ○ No

5. Comments:

APPENDIX 2. Questions for Transcript Analysis

<u>Technology</u>

1. What level of connection was made? (5 pt. max.)

   1. No connection between library and caller
   2. Chat only
   3. Basic queue
   4. Interactive, but some databases failed to work in LIVE
   5. Interactive, with full co-browsing

   No connection between library and caller.

       This usually happens when the caller disconnects before the library staff member picks up her/his call, or when the software fails during the connection process. We have had significant problems with this type of event. The caller often tries again, but sometimes fills in the exit survey first.

   Chat only

       Sometimes we have a caller with an Interactive-capable connection, but the co-browsing feature in LIVE fails to work. We can chat with the caller, but cannot push pages or co-browse.

   Basic queue

       If a caller is using a Mac, or a slow modem, the connection will revert to a Basic queue. In this mode, we can chat, push pages, and escort callers in co-browsing sessions, but escorting does not automatically load with each session.

   Interactive, but some databases failed to work in LIVE

       In this case, the interactive co-browsing worked in general, but some databases were not useable while co-browsing. WebSpirs databases have been troublesome here, as were Ebsco databases for a time.

   Interactive, with full co-browsing

       In this case, everything worked as it should, and the software was used to its fullest potential to answer the question at hand.

2. What was the session duration? (no pt. value assigned)

   1. 1-5 minutes
   2. 5-10 minutes
   3. 10-15 minutes
   4. 15-20 minutes
   5. 20-25 minutes
   6. 25-30 minutes
   7. 30+ minutes

   While an unhurried, well-paced session is certainly valued, the session duration can be attributed to many other factors, including lag time, and distractions for the caller. Sometimes, after a pause of many minutes, callers will apologize for having left to answer the door, attend to a child or make a snack. Although we assign values to the possible answers for this question, we do not include them in our tallies.

3. How was the session ended? (4 pt. max.)

   1. By library staff member, abruptly (caller had another question)
   2. By caller, abruptly (library staff member had not finished)
   3. By caller, with closing comments
   4. By library staff member, with closing comments

APPENDIX 2 (continued)

Durrance's *Willingness to Return Study* includes a scrutiny of the ways in which reference sessions are ended, and describes circumstances of closure as functional and dysfunctional. Functional closure is, she states, an element of successful reference transactions, and most often includes a clear indication regarding the user's next step and an invitation to return for more help. Dysfunctional closure is the abrupt dismissal of a user, usually without determining that he or she has been helped sufficiently.

In virtual reference, closure is complicated by some technical considerations. We can, in our LIVE service, leave a user with a list of citations to peruse *after* the session has ended, but only if the library staff member closes the session before the user does. It is sometimes difficult to ensure that the user's question has been answered and perform the closure before the user ends the session himself, with a quick "This is great, thanks." If the user manages to close the session first, any citations found during a co-browsing session will be lost to him. For this reason, we assign the highest value to closures in which the library staff member is able to ascertain completion and close the session.

By library staff member, abruptly

Transcript reveals that the caller had not finished asking questions when the library staff member terminated the session.

By caller, abruptly

Caller terminated the session before the library staff member could finish providing information.

By caller, with closing comments

Caller indicated in transcript that he/she gained sufficient information to close the session, and then did so.

By library staff member, with closing comments

Transcript reveals that both library staff member and caller felt session was complete, and staff member was able to leave patron in co-browsing session by closing first.

Reference Practices

4. Was a reference interview conducted? (4 pt. max.)

1. No, but needed
2. Yes, but over the duration of the call, after some false leads
3. No, but not needed
4. Yes, at the outset of the call

No, but needed

The session would have benefited from a clarification of the question, a discussion of sources already investigated, or a reiteration of the caller's needs. These, however, did not take place.

Yes, but over the duration of the call, after some false leads

After an initial failure to conduct a reference interview, the library staff member made one or a series of false starts before requesting clarification. This interview is done piecemeal, as missing information becomes evident.

No, but not needed

Some questions are so well worded and complete, that an interview would lead to redundancy. Others are not research-based but deal instead with housekeeping or technical details (i.e., How many books can I sign out at one time? What is my barcode number?).

Yes, at the outset of the call

An interview is conducted at the beginning of the call, which makes the caller's needs clear from the start.

5. Was the question Factual or Sources in nature?

We distinguish between Factual and Sources questions in order to set aside Sources questions for evaluation with Question #5. Otherwise, we assign no value to the two types.

6. If Sources, did the library staff member take the caller to the required resource, or simply give directions to it? (3 pt. max.)

1. Gave scant directions
2. Gave directions, to be followed simultaneously in another browser window
3. Co-browsed to the resource

This question reflects Durrance's (1995) model, "Not just question answering, but walking, pointing, instructing, and (finally) question answering." However, sometimes our virtual reference software is not compatible with the database used during the session, and the library staff member must give instructions to be followed by the caller in a separate browser window.

Gave scant directions

Library staff member named a particular resource, but did not show the caller how to use it.

Gave directions, to be followed simultaneously in another browser window

Caller was directed to a site and directed to use resource via synchronous communication while performing search in another browser window.

Co-browsed to the resource

Caller and library staff member co-browsed to resource and used it together.

7. Which tier, as described in HIL Tiered Reference service model, does this question address?

1. Tier 1
2. Tier 2
3. Tier 3

Our virtual reference service is operated under the same, tiered reference model we use to guide service at the Information Desk in face-to-face reference. Tier 1 questions are generally directional, and should be answerable by all library staff. Tier 2 questions include informational questions, requests for assistance with the Reference collection, the catalogue, online databases or other digital resources, style guides, library policies, and any information provided on the library's web site. Tier 3 questions are those that should be directed to a subject specialist within the library. These questions are either beyond the library staff member's knowledge in a given subject area, or are posed by faculty members, graduate students, or visiting scholars who need advanced assistance in a specific area.

8. Given the service expectations at this tier level, was the question completely and accurately answered? (3 pt. max.)

1. Inaccurate and incomplete
2. Accurate, but incomplete
3. Accurate and complete

Given that the greatest number of sessions dealt with sources-type questions, we based our classifications on rather broad criteria, to allow for individual differences for providing reference service. Our emphasis is on directing the user to the appropriate tool for sources-type questions, and instructing him or her on the best use of that tool and how to interpret results from any search. We also considered the same types of factors as Lancaster (1984) in determining the answerability of any given question, with greatest emphasis on his collection factors, librarian factors, and question related factors.

APPENDIX 2 (continued)

Inaccurate and incomplete

Library staff member's response included serious inaccuracies and was missing essential information.

Accurate, but incomplete

The information provided was accurate, but some important component was missing from the session.

Accurate and complete

The answer included all that might reasonably be expected in service at this tier level.

Communication Level

9. What level of written communication did the caller demonstrate? This question addresses clarity, explanation of problem, etc. (4 pt. max.)

   1. Inadequate
   2. Weak
   3. Adequate
   4. Competent

In virtual reference the quality of both the caller and the library staff member's written communication is an essential factor in measuring success. Without eye contact, visual cues, gestures, or tone of voice, virtual communication is entirely dependent upon clear and responsive writing. Yet chat is a hybrid form of communication, neither speech nor writing per se (Crystal, 2001). Experienced online chatters can confound a librarian with what Crystal describes as Netspeak's unique language, with truncated sentences, abbreviated words, "colloquial elisions" (*r u there?*), nonce formations and word play. Those who are new to online chatting tend to attempt formal written communication, creating long delays as they compose paragraphs. These callers are confused by the leapfrog pattern of online conversations, in which the participants' postings overlap each other, and traditional conversational turn taking is lost.

Inadequate

Caller used poor written communication skills, failed to convey question clearly, did not respond to queries by library staff member.

Weak

Marginal communication, overuse of abbreviations, spelling and grammatical errors impeded communication.

Adequate

Although still lacking, caller made needs known and responded to queries clearly.

Competent

Caller used written communication effectively, described problem clearly.

10. What level of written communication did the library staff member demonstrate? This question addresses clarity, explanation of resources, etc.? (4 pt. max.)

    1. Inadequate
    2. Weak
    3. Adequate
    4. Competent

Inadequate

Library staff member used poor written communication skills, failed to convey information clearly, did not respond to comments by caller.

Weak

Marginal communication, overuse of abbreviations, spelling and grammatical errors impeded communication.

Adequate

Although still lacking, library staff member conveyed information to caller, and responded to queries clearly.

Competent

Library staff member used written communication effectively, described complex material clearly.

11. Overall, what is the level of communication between the two parties? (4 pt. max.)

1. No communication
2. Poor communication–at cross purposes, not responding effectively
3. Fair communication–cross-purposes resolved
4. Good communication–both parties seem to comprehend each other

No communication

No connection between caller and library.

Poor communication

Library staff member and caller are talking at cross-purposes, and not responding to each other's comments or questions.

Fair communication

Cross-purposes may be resolved, but one party seems unable to comprehend query or instructions or is unaware of essential background information that is not being conveyed in the session.

Good communication

Both parties are communicating effectively.

General

12. Was an expression of thanks made by the caller during the session? (2 pt. max.)

1. No
2. Yes

Here, we are looking for some verification of satisfaction before the exit survey is completed.

13. What is your overall assessment of the session? How do you think both parties felt at its close? Factor in the quality of the information provided. (4 pt. max.)

1. Unsatisfactory
2. Marginally satisfactory
3. Satisfactory
4. Highly satisfactory

In this question we are trying to establish an overall score for the session, without emphasizing any one aspect.

Evaluating a Chat Reference Service at the University of South Alabama's Baugh Biomedical Library

Clista C. Clanton
Geneva B. Staggs
Thomas L. Williams

SUMMARY. The University of South Alabama's Baugh Biomedical Library recently initiated a chat reference service targeted at distance education students in the biomedical sciences. After one year of service, the library conducted an evaluation of the chat reference to assess the success of this mode of reference service. Both traditional reference and digital reference evaluation methods are selected. The evaluation measures include both statistical and descriptive data, such as: number of questions received, time and day of week questions are received, type of questions, number of users, number of repeat users, saturation rate, transcript analysis, and user surveys. Results indicate that the chat reference service is well received by both the target audience and other users. *[Article copies available for a fee from The Haworth Document Delivery Service:*

Clista C. Clanton is Web Development and Education Librarian (E-mail: cclanton@bbl.usouthal.edu); Geneva B. Staggs is Coordinator of the Medical Center Site (E-mail: gbush@jaguar1.usouthal.edu); and Thomas L. Williams is Director, Baugh Biomedical Library (E-mail: twilliam@bbl.usouthal.edu), all at the University of South Alabama, Mobile, AL 36688.

[Haworth co-indexing entry note]: "Evaluating a Chat Reference Service at the University of South Alabama's Baugh Biomedical Library." Clanton, Clista C., Geneva B. Staggs, and Thomas L. Williams. Co-published simultaneously in *Public Services Quarterly* (The Haworth Information Press, an imprint of The Haworth Press, Inc.) Vol. 2, No. 2/3, 2006, pp. 107-125; and: *Reference Assessment and Evaluation* (ed: Tom Diamond, and Mark Sanders) The Haworth Information Press, an imprint of The Haworth Press, Inc., 2006, pp. 107-125. Single or multiple copies of this article are available for a fee from The Haworth Document Delivery Service [1-800-HAWORTH, 9:00 a.m. - 5:00 p.m. (EST). E-mail address: docdelivery@haworthpress.com].

Available online at http://www.haworthpress.com/web/PSQ
© 2006 by The Haworth Press, Inc. All rights reserved.
doi:10.1300/J295v02n02_08

1-800-HAWORTH. E-mail address: <docdelivery@haworthpress.com> Website: <http://www.haworthpress.com> © 2006 by The Haworth Press, Inc. All rights reserved.]

KEYWORDS. Reference, medical libraries, distance education, virtual reference

INTRODUCTION

While still a relatively new development in reference services, virtual or digital reference is becoming more common in many libraries. One definition of virtual reference is "reference service initiated electronically, often in real-time, where users employ computers or other Internet technology to communicate with librarians, without being physically present" (MARS Digital Reference Guidelines Ad Hoc Committee, 2004). The types of technology used for virtual reference include chat, videoconferencing, Voice over IP, e-mail, and instant messaging. The use of electronic resources to answer reference questions is not considered of itself virtual reference, although online resources are often used in providing virtual reference. Furthermore, virtual reference questions are often followed-up by other modes of communication that are not considered virtual, such as telephone, fax, and regular mail.

As more libraries implement virtual reference services, evaluating these services becomes increasingly important. What constitutes a successful virtual reference service? Is it possible, or even desirable, to evaluate a virtual reference service using the tools and measures developed to evaluate traditional reference services? This paper explores some of the different methods available for evaluating a chat reference service and reports the data gathered in an evaluation of the University of South Alabama's (USA) Baugh Biomedical Library's chat reference service.

LITERATURE REVIEW

Many academic libraries have offered e-mail reference services for several years, but chat reference services are still a relatively new development. A 2001 survey of 70 Academic Research Libraries (ARL)

found that almost all (99%) offered e-mail reference, with only 29% offering chat reference (Tenopir, 2001). In July of 2002, ARL distributed another survey to 124 ARL member libraries that focused specifically on chat reference. Of the sixty-six libraries (53%) that responded to the survey, only 36 reported that they offered some sort of chat reference service. Most of these chat reference services had operated for less than two years (Ronan, 2002). A survey conducted in April of 2001 of both public and academic libraries reported 272 libraries with a chat reference service in place, with 77% of these libraries providing chat reference as part of a consortium agreement. Most of these chat services are not designed to replace e-mail or web form reference; the libraries offered the services only during limited number of hours per week (Francoeur, 2001). Within medical school libraries, 102 (87%) used digital e-mail reference services, and 25 (21%) offered chat reference in the fall of 2002, with many more planning to start chat services in 2003 (Dee, 2003).

JoAnn Sears (2001) noted in her analysis of a chat reference service that many of the articles published on virtual reference services are survey articles that discuss what various libraries are doing in this area, implementation articles describing the projects done at specific libraries or consortia, or forecast articles discussing how chat technology will impact the future of reference services. Due to the relative newness of virtual reference services, there is little in the professional literature showing formal evaluations of chat reference services, although for several years now there have been calls for libraries to evaluate their electronic reference services and then widely disseminate their results (Novotny, 2001).

BACKGROUND

The University of South Alabama's Baugh Biomedical Library began offering a virtual chat reference service in July of 2003. Initially, this service targeted distance education students, a growing segment of the biomedical student population, particularly in the College of Nursing. From 1999 through 2003, the number of online enrollments in the College of Nursing increased 350% and the number of online classes increased 380% (Tables 1 and 2).

Distance education students often face unique challenges due to their lack of access to on-campus resources, particularly the library. However, national trends indicate that even local students are less likely to visit their library than in the past. One survey of undergraduate and

TABLE 1. College of Nursing Online Enrollments

Year	Graduate	Undergraduate	Total
1999-2000	510	282	792
2000-2001	1200	671	1871
2001-2002	2108	768	2876
2002-2003	2225	579	2804

TABLE 2. College of Nursing Online Courses

Year	Graduate	Undergraduate	Total
1999-2000	10	20	30
2000-2001	30	27	57
2001-2002	51	30	81
2002-2003	84	30	114

graduate students conducted by the University of Maryland University College (UMUC) showed that 66 percent of respondents reported they "seldom" or "never" visited a library. This represents a greater percentage of students reporting they "seldom" or "never" visit a library than a previous survey conducted by UMUC in 1996, where 48 percent of respondents reported they "seldom" or "never" visited a library.

The same survey by UMUC reported that 51.2 percent of respondents indicated that off-campus access to full-text materials in the library's databases was the most useful service, while the second most useful service (51.1%) was off-campus access to the library's online catalog (Kelley & Orr, 2003). These findings are probably no surprise to most librarians and reflect the growing expectation that library users have for locating resources online. However, even providing a resource online is no guarantee that the student will be able to access it due to the often Herculean technical issues that can arise. Something as simple as the browser version or the browser's security setting can often determine if a database will successfully operate. Often, all the user experiences is the frustration of being denied access to something that the library tells them they can use.

Librarians staffing the reference desk at the University of South Alabama's biomedical library noticed an increasing number of phone calls and e-mails from distraught online students who were experiencing numerous problems in both identifying and accessing the appropriate library resources to complete their assignments. A phone survey conducted in March of 2003 of the distance education students who called the reference desk seeking help also indicated that course instructors primarily told their students to contact the nursing library liaison when they needed help using the online library resources. While having a primary point of contact is better than nothing, it is not ideal due to the increasing numbers of students needing help and the subsequent burden placed on one librarian. The students also voiced their frustration with learning how to use a computer and finding full-text articles online. The biomedical library does not provide a toll-free number for patrons to use, so students called long distance, an added expense that many students cannot afford.

After looking at options for increasing outreach to distance education students, the library decided to implement a chat reference service. Ultimately, the biomedical library selected LivePerson from several commercial products as the software for the new chat reference service. The main factors influencing the choice of LivePerson included cost, ease of use, and responsiveness of their customer service department to technical questions. The library decided to staff the chat reference service from the main reference desk during the hours of 8:00 a.m-11:45 p.m. Monday through Thursday, 8:00 a.m.-5:45 p.m. Friday and Saturday, and 1:00 p.m.-8:00 p.m. on Sundays. The hours are reduced during the summer semester, due to the library's reduced hours of operation.

To publicize this new service, library staff demonstrated LivePerson during a College of Nursing faculty workshop and an article appeared in the library's newsletter that goes out to all health science faculty at the university. Additionally, staff members highlighted and demonstrated the chat reference service during student orientations or bibliographic instruction classes. The button to initiate a chat is placed on several key pages within the library's website, including the homepage, the distance education web page, and the College of Medicine's computer lab web page, which is located within the library. Later, the chat reference became available to the clinical staff of eleven participating hospitals and clinics located in nine counties in the South Alabama rural area as part of the South Alabama Medical Network Digital Library (SAMNet), funded by a National Library of Medicine's Internet Access to Digital Library grant. A link to the chat service also appeared on the SAMNet web page, with the message that participating institutions could contact the University of South Alabama's biomedical library using live chat when a reference librarian staffed the reference desk by clicking on the chat button link.

METHODOLGY AND EVALUATION

Guidelines for virtual reference services recommend analyzing virtual reference services on a regular basis in order to evaluate their effectiveness and efficiency, utilizing input from both staff and patrons. Suggested evaluation methods include evaluating transcripts for accuracy and tone, use statistics, and user feedback, with the evaluation of the virtual reference services being at least equivalent to the regular evaluation of the library's other reference services (MARS Digital Reference Guidelines Ad Hoc Committee, 2004). It is helpful to have a benchmark with which to compare the statistics that are gathered. The most common statistics reported in the evaluations available for review are number of chat sessions, number of questions asked, and type of questions asked. However, until more evaluations are available for comparison, it is hard to determine with what to compare institutional statistics. Factors such as the number of potential users versus the number of actual users might be a good measure to know in order to make valid comparisons, but that measure is not usually included in the chat service evaluations available. The biomedical library at the University of South Alabama has a potential user base of 2,852 FTE students and 316 College of Medicine, Nursing, and Allied Health faculty.

Some of the measures used to evaluate the traditional reference services are useful and can be adopted for digital reference. However, one work in particular identifies additional ways to evaluate the data available from digital reference transactions. The manual, *Statistics, Measures and Quality Standards for Assessing Digital Reference Library Services: Guidelines and Procedures*, arose from a project, Assessing Quality in Digital Reference, supported by various public, academic, and state libraries in both the United States and the United Kingdom. The authors conducted a literature review on the evaluation of digital reference services and made site visits to various participating libraries to identify issues and approaches for the evaluation process of digital reference services. The initial draft manual was field tested in a number of libraries participating in the project, leading to the re-drafted, reviewed, and final version of the manual (McClure, Lankes, Gross, & Choltco-Devlin, 2002). The manual is presented as a first step in an ongoing process to develop statistics, measures, and quality standards by which to assess and improve digital reference services, with the authors encouraging others to build upon the manual with their own assessment work.

While *Statistics, Measures and Quality Standards for Assessing Digital Reference Library Services: Guidelines and Procedures* gives multiple ways of measuring digital reference services, the authors recognize that not all of these statistics and measures would be appropriate for an individual library, and that users should choose those that will be the most meaningful or relevant for their situation. Of interest to our library are the number of questions received, the times when chats are initiated, the number of repeat users, and the input users provided via the post-chat survey. Since LivePerson has an administrative feature that allows for transcript searching, these particular measures are easy to gather. Transcripts are stored on LivePerson's server for a one-year rolling period. Once a transcript is retrieved, the information available within the transcript includes start date and time of the chat, duration of the chat, the name of the librarian who handled the chat, who disconnected the chat, what browser the person initiating the chat was using, the IP address of the user, and answers to the post-chat user survey. Table 3 lists the descriptive statistics and measures chosen for our analysis in which the chat results are tabulated with a numerical value.

To place the biomedical library's chat reference statistics in proper context, it is helpful to know the reference activity levels from the reference desk and e-mail reference services. Statistics for the reference desk and the e-mail reference are compiled using a sampling methodology. Actual statistics are collected 7 different times for each day of the week the library is open, for a total of 49 days at the campus branch of the li-

TABLE 3. Chat Reference Statistics for July 2003-June 2004

Measure	Calculation	Results
Number of chat reference questions received.	Count the number of chat reference questions received.	202
Number of chat reference sessions.	Count the number of actual chat sessions.	264
Number of questions received via chat but not answered or responded to by completely digital means.	Count the number of questions received digitally but not answered or responded to by completely digital means.	21
Number of chats initiated in which no question was asked.	Count the number of chats initiated but no questions were asked.	76
Total number of users.	Count the number of users.	160
Repeat users.	Count the number of repeat users.	42
Saturation rate.	Divide the number of chat reference service users by the total target population and multiply by 100.	5%

brary, 42 days at the University Medical Center's library branch, and 35 days at the Children & Women's hospital library branch for the fiscal year (October 1-September 30). These actual numbers are divided by the number of survey days and then multiplied by the number of days the library is open. From October 2002 to September 2003, all biomedical library branches received 3,269 questions (ready reference, extended reference, or instructional) at the reference desk. Directional questions are not counted in the reference statistics, but are included in the chat reference statistics in order to determine if the service is being used for more simple or complex questions. For 2002-2003, the reference e-mail account received 68 questions, quite a drop from the 207 questions received the previous year. The reason for this fall off in questions received via e-mail reference is unclear, as the 2003-2004 statistics show 173 questions received during the ten-month period for which statistics are available.

McClure et al. (2002) define a digital reference transaction as "one in which all communication between the user and staff is conducted electronically or digitally." Therefore, a digital reference question would only be counted as such if the entire transaction is conducted digitally. In other words, the question must not only be received digitally, but all responses, including the answer, must be sent digitally. This distinction is made in order to provide a measure of control and consistency in the assessment process, rather than as a belief that hybrid transactions are not on the same level as digital reference transactions. This distinction can also potentially identify the types of questions or interactions that may require more than just a digital response. When analyzing the transcripts of the chats, in 21 of the chats (8%), the librarians suggested that they call the patron rather than continuing the chat in order to answer the question. The reasons for this appeared to be lengthy chats (greater than 30 minutes), users that had re-initiated a chat to ask another question or to resolve continuing difficulties, questions that involved a technical or computer problem, and questions that involved getting information from another library department.

Table 4 shows the types of questions received through the chat reference service from July of 2003 through June of 2004. The Public Services Department Head and a reference librarian examined the chat transcripts and each counted the number of questions asked in each chat session and assigned them to their categories. The question type categories are directional, instructional, ready reference, extended reference, and training or demonstrations of the chat reference. Directional questions include questions that require directions to something or some-

TABLE 4. Chat Questions by Type

	7/03	8/03	9/03	10/03	11/03	12/03	1/04	2/04	3/04	4/04	5/04	6/04	Total
Directional	0	1	5	3	2	0	4	11	3	4	1	4	38
Instructional	0	0	4	6	2	0	4	10	0	0	1	2	29
Ready Reference	1	0	11	7	8	0	13	17	2	7	1	6	73
Extended Reference	2	2	4	13	1	0	5	14	3	10	2	6	62
Training/Demos	4	4	4	4	0	1	0	1	3	0	2	4	27
Total # of Questions	7	7	28	33	13	1	26	53	11	21	7	22	229

where. Instructional questions involve explaining how to use library resources, such as how to search the online catalog or a database. Ready reference questions are information requests requiring knowledge, use, recommendations, or interpretation of one or more sources by a member of the library staff that takes less than 10 minutes to complete; this time frame expanded from 5 minutes for our regular reference classifications to reflect the greater amount of time that chat reference often requires in answering a question. Extended reference questions are the same as ready reference but require more than 10 minutes to answer. Training and demonstrations include staff training on the chat reference software and demonstrations of the service to different user groups.

Another measure is usage of the chat reference by time of day, which is useful in determining peak or slower usage times. If the chat or digital reference service can only be staffed during certain hours, this type of analysis can be quite helpful in choosing when to offer the service. Our peak usage period occurred between 8:00 a.m. and 4:00 p.m., with 73% of the chats being initiated (Figure 1). The most popular times for chats to be initiated were 10:00 a.m. -12:00 p.m. and 2:00 p.m. and 4:00 p.m., which corresponds closely to what the University of California in Irvine found when they evaluated their electronic (e-mail) reference service (Horn & Kjaer, 2000). Their three most popular times for questions were 10:00 a.m. to 12:00 p.m., 12:00 p.m. to 2:00 p.m., and 2:00 p.m. to 4:00 p.m., also the busiest time periods at their reference desk. Usage of the chat reference service at the biomedical library dropped markedly in the evening hours, with no chats being initiated after 11:00 p.m., although the service is staffed until 11:45 p.m.

The reference desk is staffed in three different shifts at the campus branch of the biomedical library (also where the chat service is staffed) between the hours of 8:00 a.m.-1:00 p.m., 1:00 p.m.-4:00 p.m., and 4:00 p.m.-12:00 a.m. Figure 2 shows usage of the chat service during the different reference shifts.

A further breakdown of the chats by day of the week shows fairly consistent use from Monday through Friday, with less use during the weekend (Figure 3).

A five question optional user survey displays in the chat window at the end of each chat. Due to some technical compatibility issues between the LivePerson software and browser types, Netscape users were not given the option of completing the survey, as it did not load at the end of the chat sessions. This reduced the number of potential surveys that could have been returned, as 17% of the chat sessions were initiated by Netscape users (n = 45). Microsoft's Internet Explorer was the

FIGURE 1. Chats by Hour of Day (n = 264)

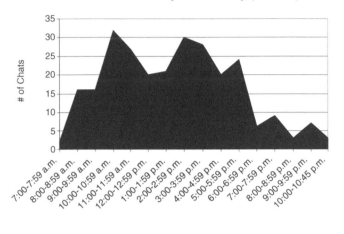

FIGURE 2. Number of Chats by Reference Shift (n = 264)

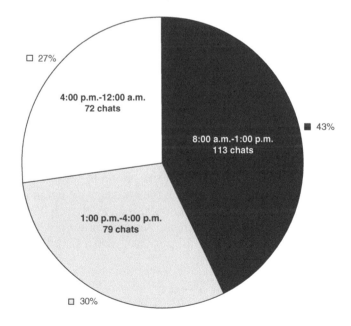

FIGURE 3. Chat Session by Day of Week (n = 264)

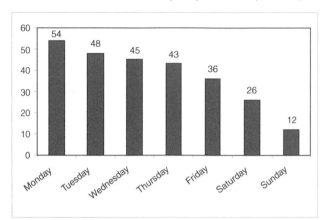

browser of choice for 81% of the chat service users (n = 214). The remaining 2% of the chat sessions (n = 5) were initiated using either ia-archiver or msnbot.

The survey questions were (1) Would you like us to e-mail you a transcript of this chat? (2) If yes, please provide your e-mail. (3) Did you find this online reference service helpful? (4) Would you use this service again? (5) Please provide any feedback you may have to help us improve this service. Twenty-seven percent of people who had a chat interaction completed the survey (n = 43). Ninety-eight percent of these people found the chat reference service helpful (n = 42). A full 100% said they would use the service again. Given that 42 of the 160 total users used the chat service more than once, this appears to have been borne out. The one person who stated that the service did not help indicated a preference for talking on the phone to someone at the library, and also indicated a desire to use the chat service again at some future point. The last survey question is designed to give chat users an avenue to express their impressions of the service, either positive or negative. The statements provided are all positive, with a sampling of them listed below:

- "This is a great help. Thanks."
- "I enjoy using the chat because the staff are always able to help me and because of them I feel like I am a more productive and successful student."

- "Always helpful. The librarians are great and I really think this program helps me as a student!"
- "This was my first time on chat with a librarian and I am thoroughly amazed and delighted that this service exists. What a wonderful resource!"
- "I think it is wonderful!"
- "Quick and informative. A wonderful service for the online student."

The completed surveys give some indication about users' satisfaction with the service, but they do not necessarily indicate service quality. An evaluation of the biomedical library's chat transcripts by the Department Head of Public Services and a reference librarian indicate that a large number (87%) of the questions are answered correctly with either the appropriate resources recommended or the actual answers given. Eight percent of the questions are either not answered or answered incorrectly, with some contributing factors including technical problems with the online source recommended that precluded getting the information needed, or disconnection of the chat by the user before the librarian gave the answer. Five percent of the questions fell into a category of "unable to determine if they were answered correctly," as either a source used seemed unclear if it would provide the answer or the chat session switched to a phone conversation, which precludes further evaluation. While this is a rather informal way of determining the correct answer rate, the transcript details of the interaction between the librarian and patron does give enough information to conduct an evaluation. The initial picture given is positive, especially if compared to the 55 percent rule. Documented by Peter Hernon and Charles McClure (1986), unobtrusive research into the effectiveness of reference showed that 55 of the questions asked in a library are answered correctly and 45 are answered incorrectly. The University of Maryland conducted a pilot study to assess the quality of services provided to chat reference users, addressing methodological concerns and providing data on which to test various analytical approaches to data analysis. While this pilot study is small, results indicated that answer accuracy is higher for chat reference than for in-library reference service (Domas, Abels, & Kaske, 2003).

Whether the high rate of questions answered correctly through the chat reference service is due to the types of questions received or the types of resources used to answer the questions is worth investigating further. Very few of the questions received required the librarian to consult print sources or multiple sources for the answer. Following are several complete transcripts that show questions answered correctly and the length of the chat session. If the user does not close their chat window, the chat time continues to accrue even if there is no more dialogue, which can contribute to lengthy chat times even if the actual dialogue is brief.

Librarian: Hi, this is XXXX. What can I help you with?
Visitor: I am looking for DNA purification techniques. Can you help?
Librarian: Sure. One moment while I locate that for you.
Librarian: Here is a page that contains some DNA purification protocols.
Librarian: http://micro.nwfsc.noaa.gov/protocols/
Librarian: Is that what you are looking for?
Visitor: yes. . . thanks for the help.
Librarian: You're welcome.
(chat session lasted 2 minutes 33 seconds)
****
Librarian: Hi, this is XXXX. What can I help you with?
Visitor: Hi. I'm XXXX. I'm a nursing grad student. I've located some articles I think I need. Just can't find full text. Can you help? I found them on Pubmed.
Librarian: What is the journal name and the year you are looking for?
Visitor: 1. Journal of Cardiovasc Nursing 2001, April 2. Prog Cardiovasc Nurs 1997 winter 3. J Am Acad Nurse Pract. 1994 Sept 4. Heart Lung 1993 Sept-Oct (is that last one a nursing journal?)
Librarian: We have the Journal of Cardiovascular Nursing online. I'll send you the page where you can look it up.
Librarian: http://atoz.ebsco.com/home.asp?Id=bblsa
Librarian: Just type in the title in the top right hand search box. Do you see it?
Visitor: yes, i'll try it. i feel like such a dummy. how did i ever get through undergrad w/o learning how to use this library??
Librarian: We only have Progress in Cardiovascular Nursing from 2000 on. You could order it via interlibrary loan. I'll send you the page for that as well.
Visitor: Wait, I have the J Cardiovasc Nurs title in front of me. Now where do I go?
Librarian: You would select the blue part, where is says "is available in."

Visitor: thanks. think I found it. now have the article titles in front of me.
Librarian: Good. I think the other two journals will not have full text on-line for the years you want.
Librarian: How soon do you need the articles?
Visitor: how would i have found this page on my on? need them by fri-day.
Librarian: From the biomedical library web site, you will see a link that says Online Journals and Books.
Visitor: ok. guess i just need to play around and do some digging.
Librarian: I don't know if interlibrary loan would be able to fill the arti-cle requests by Friday. It's possible that if we own the print version, they could do it. Would you like the link for the form?
Visitor: please
Librarian: http://southmed.usouthal.edu/library/docdel/forms/illform.html
Librarian: This is available from the library's web site, under Interli-brary Loan.
Librarian: If you haven't searched in the EBSCO databases, you may want to try that. They have a nursing collection that has a lot of full text in it.
Librarian: Would you like the link for that?
Visitor: thanks so much for your help.
Librarian: Would you like the link for EBSCO?
Visitor: yes, please.
Librarian: http://southmed.usouthal.edu/library/resources/index.htm
Librarian: Select EBSCO databases from the list, then scroll down until you see HealthSource:Nursing/Academic Edition.
Visitor: thank you.
Librarian: Let me know if you need anything else. This service is staffed until about 11:45 p.m.
Visitor: thanks. I'll probably be back!! Nice to know you're there!
Librarian: You are welcome!
(chat session lasted 53 minutes 19 seconds)

On the following page is a transcript of a question that was answered incorrectly by recommending the wrong website. The person answering the question was unaware of the class website that had been developed by one of the biomedical librarians for a class in the College of Medi-cine, pointing to the need for better communication between the mem-bers of the reference staff. Since contacting users after they have disconnected from a chat is not possible unless they elect to leave their e-mail address, correcting wrong answers or addressing technical issues has been difficult. Occasionally, the librarian will ask for contact information within the chat if they know that an issue can be addressed by another librarian or systems staff person, but this pre-supposes that the librarian is aware that they cannot answer the question, as opposed to having supplied the wrong information.

Librarian: how may i help you?
Visitor: I am a current medical student at USACOM
Visitor: im looking for the web site for a class
Visitor: Public health requires to learn how to utilize the resources at Biomedical library
Librarian: did you look on the com home page?
Visitor: i think the web page is through biomedical library
Visitor: it has questions that we are suppose to find the answers for by using OVID and other resources
Librarian: is this that class with XXXX
Visitor: i believe so
Librarian: hold on let me see if a see a copy laying around.
Librarian: keeping holding please.
Visitor: sure
Librarian: try this site: www.epibiostat.ucsf.edu/epidem/epidem.html
Visitor: thank you
(chat session lasted 15 minutes and 33 seconds)

   One of the unique aspects of both e-mail and chat reference is the availability of a written record of the transaction, allowing for evaluations of reference service, the librarian's reference skills, and the most common requests or problems of the chat service population. In reading the transcripts of the first year's chats, this reveals that students are evidently confused about how to locate full-text articles when conducting a bibliographic citation database search. Some of the databases the library subscribes to allow for local holding notes, which the students translated as "available full-text online right here right now through this screen," when in reality they needed to access the journal from the list of electronic journals through a different link on the library's website. Distance education students' access to full-text online resources is crucial, and for many other users full-text online is the preferred way of accessing materials even if they have access to print holdings. The library provides access to approximately 3,500 electronic journals and 300 electronic books, but if the students are having a difficult time locating the content of these journals, the problem goes beyond availability. Future plans are to include more bibliographic instruction and an online tutorial on how to locate the various full-text online resources to which the library subscribes.

An analysis of the biomedical library's transcripts also helped the librarian overseeing the service realize that certain useful features of the software are being underutilized by some of the librarians, such as pushing web pages or search results directly to the user. Now that there is an awareness of the common questions asked by the users, the canned responses feature in LivePerson can also be more fully developed. For example, one common problem involves users trying to access the library's resources using Internet Explorer 6 or higher. If the privacy setting is at too high of a level, some library electronic resources do not work properly. A canned response can be created to send the information on how to change the privacy setting at the push of the button, saving both typing time for the librarian and waiting time for the user. The canned response might read: "For some reason, Internet Explorer 6 defaults to a higher level of security for cookies than the databases can accept. To change this: From the menu at the top of IE, select *Tools*, then select *Internet Options*, then select the *Privacy* tab. This is probably set to *Medium*; change to the *Low* setting. You may need to exit Internet Explorer and open it again."

CONCLUSION

What constitutes a successful chat reference service? Is it the number of questions received by the service? Is it the number of users or repeat users of the service? Evaluations of chat reference services thus far, especially those used in academic libraries, have not indicated a high volume of questions received or people using the service. Perhaps any evaluation undertaken should be viewed from the frame point of why the library decided to offer the service. The University of South Alabama's Baugh Biomedical Library recognized a growing underserved segment of library users, distance education students within the College of Nursing. The chat reference service potentially provided a way to reach these students with library services and resources. While the library does not require users of the chat service to identify themselves at logon by department or college, many of the users identify themselves within the chat, and a clear majority are distance education students. Over a quarter of the people using the service are repeat users, and the comments from within the chats and from the user surveys indicate a high level of satisfaction with this communication mode. From that frame point, the chat reference service is a resounding success.

Additionally, the chat reference service allowed the library to have a much clearer awareness of the issues that face remote users in both identifying and using the library's resources. This awareness enabled the library to create new tools such as web tutorials in both HTML and PowerPoint that address many of the remote users' common questions. Future plans for web tutorials include developing multimedia (audio and video) tutorials that will instruct the user on how to conduct database searches, how to locate full-text articles online, and how to fix common technical computer problems. These online tutorials will supply our distance education students with the information that our on-campus students already receive via various library instruction classes and assignments.

As online students contact the library with their course assignments, it has also become increasingly evident that not only do we need to educate the students about what the library can and cannot do for them, but we need to educate their course instructors as well. Some online instructors have been directing students to supply hyperlinks or URLs to full-text articles for assignments so that the instructor can also retrieve the article, which is not always possible with the databases being used. Not surprisingly, something that appears straightforward from the instructor's point of view causes much frustration to students who have been unable to comply due to technical issues outside of their scope. Backhus and Summey (2003) recommend that librarians work with the online course faculty throughout the course cycle, beginning with the creation of the course in order to integrate library-related activities and assignments and ending with course evaluations. Plans are currently being made by the biomedical library's education coordinator to offer instruction on the library's resources and services to the online course faculty, a segment of the university that has thus far proven elusive to reach and educate. This type of outreach and collaboration can only serve to better inform both course instructors and librarians on how to more fully serve a growing segment of the university's and the library's student population.

REFERENCES

Backhus, S. H., & Summey, T. P. (2003). Collaboration: The key to unlocking the dilemma of distance reference services. *The Reference Librarian*, 83/84, 193-202.

Dee, C. R. (2003). Chat reference service in medical libraries: Part 2–trends in medical school libraries. *Medical Reference Services Quarterly, 22*(2), 15-28.

Domas, White M., Abels, E. G., & Kaske N. (2003). Evaluation of chat reference service quality: Pilot study. *D-Lib Magazine, 9*(2). Retrieved August 16, 2004, from http://www.dlib.org/dlib/february03/white/02white.html.

Francoeur, S. (2001). An analytical survey of chat reference services. *Reference Services Review, 29*(3), 189-203.

Hernon, P., & McClure, C. R. (1986). Unobtrusive reference testing: The 55 percent rule. *Library Journal, 111*(7), 37-41.

Horn, J., & Kjaer, K. (2000). Evaluating the "Ask a Question" service at the University of California, Irvine. In R. D. Lankes, J. W. Collins III, & A. S. Kasowitz (Eds.), *Digital reference service in the new millennium: Planning, management, and evaluation* (pp. 135-145). New York: Neal-Shuman.

Kelley, K. B., & Orr, G. J. (2003). Trends in distant student use of electronic resources: A survey. *College & Research Libraries, 64*(3), 176-191.

Machine-Assisted Reference Section (MARS) Digital Reference Guidelines Ad Hoc Committee, Reference and User Services Association (2004). Guidelines for implementing and maintaining virtual reference services. *Reference & User Services Quarterly, 44*(1), 9-13.

McClure, C. R., Lankes, R. D., Gross, M., & Choltco-Devlin, B. (2002). *Statistics, measures and quality standards for assessing digital reference library services: Guidelines and procedures.* Syracuse, NY: Syracuse University, Information Institute of Syracuse.

Novotny, E. (2001). Evaluating electronic reference services: Issues, approaches and criteria. *The Reference Librarian*, 74, 103-120.

Ronan, J., & Turner, C. (2002). *Chat Reference.* SPEC kit 273. Washington, D.C.: Association of Research Libraries, Office of Leadership and Management Services.

Sears, J. A. (2001). Chat reference service: An analysis of one semester's data. *Issues in Science and Technology Librarianship.* Retrieved August 15, 2004, from http://www.istl.org/01-fall/article2.html.

Tenopir, C. (2001). Virtual reference services in a real world. *Library Journal, 126*(12), 38-40.

The University of Texas at Arlington's Virtual Reference Service: An Evaluation by the Reference Staff

Katherine D. Casebier

SUMMARY. The University of Texas at Arlington's Library began using an online chat reference in 2002. The service, called Collaborative Digital Reference Service, later became "Ask a Librarian." Slightly over one year later, the library joined the University of Texas System's "Ask a Librarian" service. Both services are powered by software suite called QuestionPoint. In May 2003 and May 2004, the library's reference staff shared their views towards this new reference tool by completing a questionnaire. Statistics and staff members' responses are analyzed in this study. *[Article copies available for a fee from The Haworth Document Delivery Service: 1-800-HAWORTH. E-mail address: <docdelivery@haworthpress.com> Website: <http://www.HaworthPress.com> © 2006 by The Haworth Press, Inc. All rights reserved.]*

Katherine D. Casebier is Assistant Professor of Library Science, Houston Baptist University, Houston, TX 77074-3298 (E-mail: dcasebier@hbu.edu). The author completed this paper while serving as a Library Assistant at the University of Texas at Arlington.

The author wishes to thank John Dillard and Karen Hopkins for their advice and the staff and librarians of the University of Texas at Arlington Libraries' Information Services department.

[Haworth co-indexing entry note]: "The University of Texas at Arlington's Virtual Reference Service: An Evaluation by the Reference Staff." Casebier, Katherine D. Co-published simultaneously in *Public Services Quarterly* (The Haworth Information Press, an imprint of The Haworth Press, Inc.) Vol. 2, No. 2/3, 2006, pp. 127-142; and: *Reference Assessment and Evaluation* (ed: Tom Diamond, and Mark Sanders) The Haworth Information Press, an imprint of The Haworth Press, Inc., 2006, pp. 127-142. Single or multiple copies of this article are available for a fee from The Haworth Document Delivery Service [1-800-HAWORTH, 9:00 a.m. - 5:00 p.m. (EST). E-mail address: docdelivery@haworthpress.com].

Available online at http://www.haworthpress.com/web/PSQ
doi:10.1300/J295v02n02_09

KEYWORDS. Academic libraries, librarian satisfaction, reference services, staff surveys, virtual reference

INTRODUCTION

Studies conducted in the business world have demonstrated the direct relationship between employee attitude and customer satisfaction. One such study by Schmit and Allscheid (1995) found that each employee's attitudes, intentions, and behaviors, whether in upper management or at the clerk level, affect customer service. It is for this reason that evaluations of staff attitudes toward library services should be conducted on a regular basis. In other words, patron usage statistics alone should not be the only criteria determining existing services. This study evaluates the University of Texas at Arlington's (UTA) Libraries' reference staff attitudes over a two-year period towards the QuestionPoint online reference chat service. The study seeks to diagnose the overall view of the reference staff and compare the findings to actual statistics gathered in 2003 and 2004.

LITERATURE REVIEW

Facing competition from the Internet and search engines such as Google, libraries are scrambling to find tools to recruit remote library users. Since many patrons will not physically come to the library, librarians are taking their resources to their customers via the Internet. One of these services, chat reference, is similar to instant messaging. As Breeding (2003, p. 38) notes, "At first blush, conversations held through instant messaging appear sloppy and chaotic, yet far more nuances of expression prevail than would be read in a typical e-mail exchange. The pervasive presence of instant messaging will be ignored only by organizations willing to risk irrelevance." This sentiment is echoed by others such as Dempsey's comment that ". . . state libraries are being threatened, branches are closing, and the Internet is luring the information-seeking public. It's imperative that you keep up with the times in order to survive" (Dempsey, 2003, p. 6).

This drive to provide library services online has changed librarians' jobs dramatically. Librarians' jobs today do not resemble librarians' jobs of yesterday, and much ambiguity has emerged. As Kniffel states, "Ambiguity means being told one thing is your job and then being forced by circumstances into another role completely. There is plenty of ambiguity going on for librarians in the Information Age, which is redefining the entire profession," (Kniffel, 1999, p. 38).

This redefining of library jobs and the need for increased technological skills has caused more stress to the library profession. Van Fleet and Wallace (2003) coined this as *technostress*, or the characteristic of a staff members' inability to handle "new computer technologies in a healthy manner" (p. 188). Van Fleet and Wallace also note that technostress breeds other feelings of dissatisfaction. These include *loss of personal identity* by distancing the user from the librarian, *loss of resources* to the patron by the librarians having to answer reference questions by electronic resources only (printed sources may not be available), and *loss of confidentiality*. QuestionPoint, the online chat service used for this study, keeps transcripts for some time with patrons' e-mail addresses, etc. Although these are only available to the library staff, they are still records which government officials might requisition (Kenney, 2002). Moreland (1993) echoes similar comments in her article, "Techno-stress and Personality Type."

These stressful situations mentioned above do not include the difficulty of conducting a reference interview via the Internet. Recalling Taylor's view that "users have to express something they don't know," (Lankes, Collins, & Kasowitz, 2000, p. 9), librarians must attempt to discover the users' needs via the reference interview. Diagnosing the users' needs accurately is not something all librarians are comfortable doing (DeHart, 1979) and doing this without visual and audio clues can be difficult. Joseph Janes studied reference staffs' attitudes concerning the use of technology through a survey of 648 public and academic reference librarians. Janes found that both academic and public libraries noted a decrease in the number of reference questions. Of the 353 responses from academic libraries, 26.2% said they received three to 10 reference questions by way of digital reference. Only 4% of these digital reference questions came to the library via chat reference (Janes, 2002).

BACKGROUND AND HISTORY

The UTA Libraries system consists of the main library (Central), two branch libraries (the Science and Engineering Library and the Architecture and Fine Art Library) and three satellite libraries (the UTA/Fort Worth Library, the Electronic Business Library, and the Social Work

Electronic Library). These libraries serve the university's approximately 25,000 students.

In order to provide reference assistance to remote affiliates, the UTA Libraries joined the Library of Congress' Collaborative Digital Reference Service (CDRS), which was launched in June 2002. Later, the service became known as "Ask a Librarian." The service uses the QuestionPoint software and is one of the *two* QuestionPoint chat services offered at the UTA Libraries System. It is referred to in this study as the "UTA Chat" and is staffed solely by UTA library employees. Its main purpose is to serve UTA students, faculty, and staff, although assistance will be given to patrons worldwide. This chat service is the subject of the May 2003 questionnaire referred to hereafter as *Questionnaire I.*

The *second* chat service the library system offers is operated through the University of Texas System and referred to as "UT System Chat." The difference between the two chats is that the UT System Chat is a collaborative effort between seven libraries in the UT System to help all students and guests. In April 2004, the seven libraries participating in the UT System Chat service are branches in Arlington, Austin, Brownsville, Dallas, Pan America, San Antonio, and the School of Public Health at the UT Health Science Center at Houston. The UT System Chat and the UTA Chat are the subjects for the 2004 questionnaire hereafter referred to as *Questionnaire II.*

METHODS

The author of this study designed a questionnaire to measure the UTA Libraries Reference department's attitudes toward the new reference service. The questionnaire consisted of 38 mostly open-ended questions, designed to encourage participants to give their opinions and attitudes towards the service. Since the study seeks to discover the attitude of the department as a whole and not only those staffing the online chat service, anyone in the department willing to complete a copy received a questionnaire. In order to discover if these attitudes varied over the course of one year, reference staff received a copy of the questionnaire via e-mail in May of 2003 and again in May of 2004.

Questionnaire I

In the spring of 2003, 10 out of 16 staff members working in Central Library completed and returned the questionnaire. During this time period, UTA only had one online chat service ("UTA Chat") manned exclusively by library staff. This service operated Monday through Thursday from 2 p.m. to 5 p.m. for a total of 15 hours. The UTA Chat service was not available over the weekend, but regular e-mail reference service was available. A copy of the questionnaire and results are available in the Appendix.

Questionnaire II

In spring 2004, the second questionnaire ("UTA System Chat"), and the same one used during the spring 2003, provided an opportunity to discover if staff's attitudes changed over the course of a year. This time, 19 out of 29 staff members from Central Library and the two branch libraries completed and returned the surveys. During 2004, the UTA Library System not only offered UTA Chat but also the UT System Chat service.

The UTA Libraries offered UTA Chat during the same hours as the year before, but the UT System Chat doubled this coverage by being available from noon to 6 p.m., Monday through Thursday and on Friday from noon to 4 p.m., for a total of 28 hours. Neither service offered coverage over the weekend, but the Libraries offered reference e-mail assistance. A copy of the questionnaire and results are available in the Appendix.

RESULTS

Questionnaire I

Respondents to the 2003 questionnaire ("UTA Chat") felt that users did not abuse the service to find easy access to homework answers. Five respondents believed that the chat tool did not serve as the best vehicle for database instruction. Most felt that QuestionPoint functioned well for *quick reference* questions but did not provide a suitable forum for *in-depth* reference questions. One staff member stated, "It works better for ready-reference but it can work with detailed reference, only if the user has the patience and is willing to stay online."

The service's main benefit and value allowed patrons to instantly contact a live librarian, meaning patrons would have an answer more quickly than by calling over the phone or contacting by e-mail. Of the five members who regularly staffed the service, 80% did not enjoy staffing QuestionPoint and 60% felt resistance to using QuestionPoint. On the other hand, 50% of those staff who did not regularly staff the chat service in 2003 felt resistance towards the service.

Staff members repeatedly complained about the slowness of the software and that, in 2003, the system "booted-out" both users and staff. As for the future, staff believed that the library should pick a target group for marketing QuestionPoint. One member expressed that QuestionPoint is a good system that needed improvement. Sixty percent of respondents did not believe that QuestionPoint enhanced reference services.

Questionnaire II

Attitudes toward QuestionPoint changed over the course of one year. Almost 66% of the staff in 2004 believed that the service enhanced or will enhance services at UTA. While some staff indicated that QuestionPoint allowed the answering of questions in a timely manner, some staff expressed concern that those staffing QuestionPoint would not refer questions to the subject specialist. Questions answered quickly are not as likely to be forwarded or referred as often as in-depth questions.

In 2004, almost 66% of the staff still believed QuestionPoint should be used for ready reference. However, it was also mentioned that more detailed assistance could be conducted via QuestionPoint if the patron was patient enough, the system does not crash, and the focus is on teaching how to research rather than taking the time to give the answers. The remaining 33% believe that QuestionPoint can be used for both purposes.

Questionnaire II reported that 10 staff members regularly staff QuestionPoint. Only 20% of these staff members indicated that they do not want to market QuestionPoint. Slightly more than 33% of those regularly staffing the chat service do not enjoy this duty, and 55% have resistance to the service. In contrast to these numbers, about 72% of those not scheduled for regular duty enjoy chat sessions. Only two of these eight members experienced resistance to using the service. One member could not reach a decision.

In 2004, staff still believed that QuestionPoint operated exceedingly slow and that librarian-to-patron transactions appeared too slowly on the corresponding screen. One staff member said that too many windows were open during most online sessions.

DISCUSSION

QuestionPoint users asked a mixture of questions in 2003 and 2004. It is doubtful that any person, whether library assistant or librarian, possesses the expertise to ably answer all the questions all the time. In this case, the patron will wait for the library chat staff on duty to consult another more knowledgeable co-worker for the answer needed or be contacted at a later date. Even though the patron has to wait for an answer, the patron would also have to wait if s/he walked to the reference area or used the telephone.

A recurring opinion in responses to both questionnaires indicates that customers have trouble following librarian instructions while using QuestionPoint. There does not seem to be a mechanism in place to insure the patrons actually get the information needed. One library staff member suggested, "I think that research skills can be taught online, but I think that it can be done only with sending out 'canned' pre-typed sample instruction examples that include questions and answers." At times, patrons repeatedly logged on again after logging off for this very reason. This indicates that those staffing QuestionPoint need to ask the patrons if extra assistance is needed by continuing the QuestionPoint transaction over the telephone or in person. If the patron is not using his/her phone line for the Internet connection, the QuestionPoint staff can move the reference interview to the phone and use the QuestionPoint software to push pages via the Internet.

Some staff members commented that the cost of QuestionPoint seems to outweigh the benefits. A PowerPoint presentation, "QuestionPoint Collaborative Reference Service, Virtual Reference: Making It Work for You" by Diane Nester Kresh, noted the initial cost for the service is $2,000 per year (Kresh, 2002).

Tables 1 and 2 summarize the benefits and disadvantages expressed by staff concerning the chat reference service.

Although most staff members serving on QuestionPoint felt that the service is not being utilized, the data indicate otherwise. Statistics collected by reference staff show that questions received via the system are on the increase. Statistics and transcripts viewed at the QuestionPoint website provided statistics for April 2003 and April 2004 (Library of Congress & OCLC, 2003).

The important issue raised by staff is the hours QuestionPoint is available. The fact that UTA not only has its own chat but also is a member of the UT System Chat adds 16 hours per week to the existing number of hours offered via UTA Chat. Most comments requested that the

TABLE 1. Staff Expressed QuestionPoint Benefits

Benefits:	Comments:
Live contact at a distance.	"Users get instant feedback."
Another means to contact the library.	"If a student is online and using the telephone line for connection and therefore cannot call the library, the patron can 'chat' with the library."
Appeals to the younger generation.	"We're trying to adjust to students comfort level by providing online assistance. They love online activities and some students are more likely to ask that way than in-person or by phone."
Makes librarians aware of needed guides, bibliographies, and special topic web pages.	

TABLE 2. Staff Expressed QuestionPoint Disadvantages

Disadvantages:	Comments:
Format is best for quick reference.	
Not the best way to handle in-depth questions. Some questions require in person instruction.	"Some need to be in the library." "The questions that come in are usually more difficult to answer. It seems to me that it takes a long time to type out a reply, send the question, and wait for the reply to come back, for both the inquirer and the staff member. Answering a question that comes in on the telephone is much more dynamic than answering a question that comes in by electronic mail."
Better to answer questions by phone.	
Not enough patrons are using it to make it worthwhile.	"It is a disadvantage to devote the time and money to QuestionPoint that UTA has for such a small return." "When I did it, it was underutilized."
Takes more time to help the patron. Slow-typing answers.	"Typing the answer is slower than giving a verbal answer. Correcting mistakes takes even longer."
No way to evaluate answers given in a timely manner.	"I think we are more apt to be concerned with answering questions quickly rather than thoroughly just by the nature of QuestionPoint."
Stress to answer patron quickly.	"It needs timely response because the user is staring at the screen waiting for an answer. The pressure is on when the staff member is trying to type fast and finding the correct answer." "Made things more hectic."
System is slow and patrons/librarians are dropped.	
Staff time spent better elsewhere.	"No, I thought that more people would be contacting us. At this time, I see QuestionPoint duty as equivalent to guard duty."
Staff attitude.	"Nobody becomes really passionate about it so it is probably really easy to develop a luke-warm attitude about it. Institutionally it says we really do not value it highly—nobody devotes their time to it but we want to add it to the list of 'bells and whistles' we provide."

hours of operation be extended or moved into the late evening hours. One staff member even suggested extending chat hours to 2 a.m.

The resistance to using the QuestionPoint software is evident. One employee wrote, "Scrap the software and get Instant Messenger." Another stated, "If people do not receive some sort of reply almost immediately, they will disconnect. I have found that people will disconnect and 'leave' without even bothering to tell you that they are disconnecting. It is almost rude, as if you and another person were at dinner, and the other person gets up and literally leaves the restaurant without telling you."

Staff members made these suggestions concerning the use of QuestionPoint:

- Hire a consultant.
- Show students examples of questions; how it can be used.
- Since UT System is now using it, marketing will take care of itself.
- Not use QuestionPoint until UTA can staff it properly.
- Drop the QuestionPoint chat service; reference e-mail is adequate.
- Let all staff members use QuestionPoint (as a test) to get feed back on the product.
- Market it in the UTA publications like the Shorthorn, UTA Today, and UTA Radio/TV. Hand out fliers in dorms, the UC, etc.
- Fix the timeout, connection problems.
- Have a bigger Question/Answer box-text box is too small to write detailed instructions.
- Change the operation hours to more evening hours–even during the night.

CONCLUSIONS AND OPPORTUNITIES FOR FURTHER RESEARCH

This study found that QuestionPoint statistics are on the rise. Patrons are using the QuestionPoint chat service as often as they are contacting reference via e-mail. The library staff has mentioned that the updated version of QuestionPoint seems to have repaired the software issues which caused patrons and staff members to be disconnected or dropped.

This study also discovered that most staff members regularly scheduled for online chat reference resisted the service. Others not regularly scheduled are eager to be added to the QuestionPoint reference roster. Is it possible that the dislike of online chat comes after many hours of waiting for a chat session that never materializes or is the problem with the format alone? The format alone does not lend itself to the give and take of an in-person interview. Is it possible the library staff member does not receive the same feeling of productivity and professional reward one receives at the reference desk or over the telephone? More research covering the attitudes of library staff members and this kind of reference interaction should be conducted. It seems to this researcher that no matter how many "bells and whistles" are added, most library workers do not enjoy this reference tool. Studies are needed to discover why most librarians prefer in-person or telephone reference interviews over reference interviews conducted via chat.

Recently, the QuestionPoint interface received a new look. The new interface has a split screen so users can see the chat session and user information at the same time. The new interface is also quicker than the older version. A new study in the year 2005 comparing the attitudes of the librarians towards this new interface and statistics for 2005 would be informative.

REFERENCES

Breeding, M. (2003). Instant messaging: It's not just for kids anymore. *Computers in Libraries, 23*(10), 38-40.

DeHart, F. E. (1979). *The librarian's psychological commitments: Human relations in librarianship.* Westport, CT: Greenwood Press.

Dempsey, K. (2003). Here's your guide to VR: Use it to stay relevant. *Computers in Libraries, 23*(4), 6.

Janes, J. (2002). Digital reference: Reference librarians' experiences and attitudes. *Journal of the American Society for Information Science and Technology, 53*(7), 549-566.

Kenney, B. (2002). Live digital reference. *Library Journal, 127*(16), 46-47.

Kniffel, L. (1999). Survey says librarians rank low in stress, hel-lo? *American Libraries, 30*(5), 38.

Kresh, D. N. (2002). Virtual reference: Making it work for you. Paper presented at the Michigan Library Consortium, April 2002. Retrieved May 25, 2005, from http://www.mlc.lib.mi.us/workshop/vendorday02/kresh_presentation/.

Lankes, R. D., Collins, III, J. W., & Kasowitz, A. S. (2000). *Digital reference service in the new millennium: Planning, management, and evaluation.* New York: Neal-Schuman.

Library of Congress & OCLC. (2003). *QuestionPoint Cooperative Virtual Reference.* Retrieved May 25, 2004, from http://www.questionpoint.org.

Moreland, V. (1993, July). Technostress and personality type. *ONLINE, 17*(4), 59-62.

Schmit, M. J., & Allscheid, S. P. (1995). Employee attitudes and customer satisfaction: Making theoretical and empirical connections. *Personal Psychology, 48*(3), 521-536.

Van Fleet, C., & Wallace, D. P. (2003). From the editors, Virtual libraries–Real threats: Technostress and virtual reference. *Reference & User Services Quarterly, 42*(3), 188-191.

APPENDIX

Questionnaire I (2003) and Questionnaire II (2004) for the Chat Reference Service

---

PATRONS:
1. Do you think patrons are asking for reasonable help or are the questions too much like doing their homework for them? Please explain. Please circle one: Reasonable help/Homework

2003	2004
NA/0/Don't Know = 2	NA/0/Don't Know = 6
Reasonable help = 7	Reasonable help = 13
Homework = None	Homework = None
Both = 1	

2. When using QuestionPoint are you able to quickly give the patron information or do most questions require more time to respond than applicable to chat reference? Please circle one
Respond Quickly   Takes More Time

2003	2004
NA/0/Don't Know = 3	NA/0/Don't Know = 5
Respond Quickly = 5	Respond Quickly = 8
Takes More Time = 2	Takes More Time = 6

3. Do you refer patrons to websites, print material in the library, and/or online services or databases?

2003	2004
NA/0/Don't Know = 3	NA/0/Don't Know = 5
Yes = 7	Yes = 14

4. Are most patrons able to follow your instructions via QuestionPoint to material online or in databases or can research skills be taught via QuestionPoint? Please explain.

2003	2004
NA/0/Don't Know = 5	NA/0/Don't Know = 9
No = 2	Yes = 10
Yes = 3	

5. What subject areas have you seen most addressed in QuestionPoint? Please name two.

2003	2004	
NA/0/Don't Know = 7	NA/0/Don't Know = 7	
See Below = 14	See Below = 12	
Subjects:	**Subjects:**	
Geography	Political Science	Law
Criminal Justice	English/literature	Social Policy
Wireless Telephone Systems	General Library	Biofeedback
Art History	History	Genealogy
Current Events	Nursing	Current-events
General Library	Business	Psychology
	Marketing	Company
	Information	

APPENDIX (continued)

YOURSELF: 6. Have you been on the QuestionPoint schedule on a regular basis and/or have reference questions been forwarded to you from someone on "QuestionPoint duty"?	
2003 NA/0/Don't Know = 1 No = 4 Regular Basis = 5	**2004** NA/0/Don't Know = 1 Regular Basis = 10 Not Regular = 8
7. What percentage of QuestionPoint questions do you refer to another library staff member? Please circle one. 5% 10% 25% 50% 75%	
2003 NA/0/Don't Know = 4 5% or less = 4 50% = 1 Never = 1	**2004** NA/0/Don't Know = 9 5% or less = 6 10% = 3 50% = 1
8. In your opinion, has the use of QuestionPoint enhanced the UTA library experience? Please explain. Please circle one: YES NO	
2003 NA/0/Don't Know = 2 No = 6 Yes = 2	**2004** NA/0/Don't Know = 1 No = 6 Yes = 12
9. Do you feel questions posted to QuestionPoint are responded to in a timely manner? Why or why not? Please circle one: YES NO	
2003 NA/0/Don't Know = 2 No = 1 Yes = 7	**2004** NA/0/Don't Know = 2 Yes = 17 No = None
10. What has been the benefit or disadvantage to using QuestionPoint as a reference tool?	
2003 NA/0/Don't Know = 2 See Below = 17	**2004** NA/0/Don't Know = 1 See Below = 18
11. How has using QuestionPoint affected your job duties?	
2003 NA/0/Don't Know = 3 No = 4 Yes = 3	**2004** NA/0/Don't Know = 5 No = 11 Yes = 3
12. Do you feel QuestionPoint is more adequate for answering ready-reference or more detailed reference questions? Does QuestionPoint work for both?	
2003 NA/0/Don't Know = 1 Ready Reference = 8 Both = 1	**2004** NA/0/Don't Know = 1 Ready Reference = 12 Both = 6
13. How does using QuestionPoint compare to using regular reference e-mail for answering and receiving questions?	
2003 NA/0/Don't Know = 1 See Below = 18	**2004** NA/0/Don't Know = None See Below = 19

14. How well do you feel QuestionPoint has been marketed?	
2003 NA/0/Don't Know = 1 Well = 4 Not well = 5	**2004** NA/0/Don't Know = 2 Well = 11 Not well = 6
15. Would you change UTA's profile in QuestionPoint?	
2003 NA/0/Don't Know = 2 No = 2 Yes = 2 Don't Understand = 4	**2004** NA/0/Don't Know = 10 No = 8 Yes = 1
16. What suggestions do you have about marketing QuestionPoint?	
2003 NA/0/Don't Know/None = 5 See Below = Five	**2004** NA/0/Don't Know = 8 See Below = 11
17. Would you willingly market QuestionPoint? Why or why not? Please circle one: YES NO	
2003 NA/0/Don't Know = 3 No = 2 Yes = 5	**2004** NA/0/Don't Know = 1 No = 6 Yes = 12
18. Have you shared how to use QuestionPoint with any other staff members? Why or why not? Please circle one: YES NO	
2003 NA/0/Don't Know = 1 No = 6 Yes = 3	**2004** NA/0/Don't Know = None No = 9 Yes = 10
19. Do you market QuestionPoint during your BIs (Bibliographic Instruction) or while doing reference? Please explain. Please circle one: YES NO	
2003 NA/0/Don't Know = 4 No = 3 Yes = 3	**2004** NA/0/Don't Know = 2 No = 10 Yes = 7
20. Do you enjoy this type of reference assistance? Please explain. Please circle one: YES NO	
2003 NA/0/Don't Know = None No = 6 Yes = 4	**2004** NA/0/Don't Know = 2 No = 3 Yes = 12 Both = 2
21. Do you have a feeling of resistance toward this type of reference service? Why? Please circle one: YES NO	
2003 NA/0/Don't Know = 1 No = 5 Yes = 4	**2004** NA/0/Don't Know = 1 No = 12 Yes = 6

APPENDIX (continued)

22. Does this service meet your expectations as a library staff member? Why? Please circle one: YES NO	
2003 NA/0/Don't Know = 1 No = 8 Yes = 1	**2004** NA/0/Don't Know = 5 No = 7 Yes = 7
23. Have you had any QuestionPoint questions that were pranks?	
2003 NA/0/Don't Know = 4, [2 added See comments] No = 5 Yes = 1	**2004** NA/0/Don't Know = 1 No = 12 Yes = 6
STATISTICS: 24. Approximately how many true QuestionPoint questions have you had per week? Please circle one: less than or equal to 5 less than or equal to 10 greater than 10	
2003 NA/0/Don't Know = 4 Less than or equal to 5 = 6	**2004** NA/0/Don't Know = 4 Less than or equal to 5 = 15
25. Approximately how many of these per month? Please circle one: less than or equal to 5 less than or equal to 10 greater than 10	
2003 NA/0/Don't Know = 4 Less than or equal to 5 = 6	**2004** NA/0/Don't Know = 4 Less than or equal to 5 = 14 Less than or equal to 10 = 1 Greater than 10 = None
26. Is the number of questions increasing from month to month? Please explain if necessary.	
2003 NA/0/Don't Know = 4 No = 5 Not on Schedule = 1	**2004** NA/0/Don't Know = 10 No = 6 Yes = 3
27. Overall are the questions difficult or easy? How much time do you spend on average answering one of these questions? Please circle one: Difficult Easy	
2003 NA/0/Don't Know = 3 Difficult = 2 (one refers all questions) Easy = 5	**2004** NA/0/Don't Know = 8 Difficult = 2 Easy = 8 Both = 1
28. Please circle one: Time Spent in minutes 5 10 15 20 30+	
2003 NA/0/Don't Know = 3 5+ = 4 10+ = 2 20+ = 1	**2004** NA/0/Don't Know = 7 5+ = 2 10+ = 4 15+ = 6 20+ = 0

29. Have you had any patrons from other schools or other countries using QuestionPoint?	
2003 NA/0/Don't Know = 6 No = 3 Yes = 1 **Comments 2003:** Sweden	**2004** NA/0/Don't Know = 8 No = 2 Yes = 9 **Comments 2004:** California & other states

TECHNOLOGY:
30. What improvements or changes would you suggest for QuestionPoint?

2003 NA/0/Don't Know = 5 See Below = 5	**2004** NA/0/Don't Know = 7 No = 5 answer See Below = 7

31. What suggestions would you make concerning the interface or how it works?

2003 NA/0/Don't Know = 7 See Below = 3	**2004** NA/0/Don't Know = 9 No = 5 See Below = 5

32. Have you had any problems with the software? Please explain. Please circle one: YES   NO

2003 NA/0/Don't Know = 4 See Below = 6	**2004** NA/0/Don't Know = 4 No = 10 Yes = 5

33. Is the software and speed sufficient for Instant Message usage? Please explain if necessary. Please circle one: YES   NO

2003 NA/0/Don't Know = 3 Yes = 3 No = 4	**2004** NA/0/Don't Know = 8 No = 4 Yes = 7

FUTURE:
34. What features does this service need that it does not offer now?

2003 NA/0/Don't Know = 7 See Below = 3	**2004** NA/0/Don't Know = 11 Fine = 1 See Below = 7

35. How can QuestionPoint usage be enhanced?

2003 NA/0/Don't Know = 9 See Below = 1	**2004** NA/0/Don't Know = 8 See Below = 11

36. What times do you think would be better?

2003 NA/0/Don't Know = 6 See Below = 4	**2004** NA/0/Don't Know = 6 See Below = 13

APPENDIX (continued)

37. Do you think the hours UTA uses this chat are conducive to reference questions and convenient to the faculty, students, and staff or more of a staffing issue? Please explain. Please circle one: YES NO	
2003 NA/0/Don't Know = 2 No = 5 Yes = 1 Staffing = 1 See Below = 1	**2004** NA/0/Don't Know = 6 No = 6 Yes = 6 Both = 1
38. Any other comments you would like to make?	
2003 NA/0/Don't Know = 9 See Below = 1	**2004** NA/0/Don't Know = 10 See Below = 9

Changes in Library Technology and Reference Desk Statistics: Is There a Relationship?

Beth Thomsett-Scott
Patricia E. Reese

SUMMARY. The incorporation of technology into library processes has tremendously impacted staff and users alike. The University of North Texas (UNT) Libraries is no exception. Sixteen years of reference statistics are analyzed to examine the relationships between the implementation of CD-ROMs and web-based resources and the number of reference questions. Gate counts and circulation statistics for recent years are also evaluated. Overall, reference statistics have been declining over the years under review. The introduction of CD-ROMs caused a rise in reference statistics for several years before the statistics decreased again. Moving the resources to a web-based format minimally affected the number of reference question numbers, although the rate of decline slowed. Gate counts are increasing in one of the libraries examined and circulation statistics are rising. Changes in gate and circulation numbers

Beth Thomsett-Scott (E-mail: bscott@library.unt.edu) and Patricia E. Reese (E-mail: preese@library.unt.edu) are Science Reference Librarians, both at University of North Texas, Denton, TX 76203-5190.

[Haworth co-indexing entry note]: "Changes in Library Technology and Reference Desk Statistics: Is There a Relationship?" Thomsett-Scott, Beth, and Patricia E. Reese. Co-published simultaneously in *Public Services Quarterly* (The Haworth Information Press, an imprint of The Haworth Press, Inc.) Vol. 2, No. 2/3, 2006, pp. 143-165; and: *Reference Assessment and Evaluation* (ed: Tom Diamond, and Mark Sanders) The Haworth Information Press, an imprint of The Haworth Press, Inc., 2006, pp. 143-165. Single or multiple copies of this article are available for a fee from The Haworth Document Delivery Service [1-800-HAWORTH, 9:00 a.m. - 5:00 p.m. (EST). E-mail address: docdelivery@haworthpress.com].

are due to factors such as increased student enrollment and increased library instruction rather than technology changes within the Libraries. *[Article copies available for a fee from The Haworth Document Delivery Service: 1-800-HAWORTH. E-mail address: <docdelivery@haworthpress.com> Website: <http://www.HaworthPress.com> © 2006 by The Haworth Press, Inc. All rights reserved.]*

KEYWORDS. Academic libraries, virtual reference, Internet, CD-ROM, technology, statistics

INTRODUCTION

There is no doubt that technology, especially the Internet, has affected our lives. Many of us utilize the Internet daily and even those who do not recognize the catch-phrases: online, dot com, and e-mail are common words in today's conversations.

Libraries and librarians are also part of the fervor. Tenopir and Ennis (2001) noted that although academic librarians have pursued automation since the 1960s, the period between 1991 and 2001 experienced the greatest amount of change. In 1991, the Internet began to emerge as a publicly available research tool and CD-ROMs began to dominate as the preferred method for accessing abstracts and indexes. Several years later, web-based library resources replaced CD-ROMs.

The Internet offers tremendous opportunities for libraries to provide users with resources such as databases and electronic journals, and to offer enhanced services, such as online reference and reference web pages. Netcraft reported 57 million web sites in its January 2005 survey (http://news.netcraft.com/archives/web_server_survey.html), and Gromov (2002) estimated there are 600 million people with connections to the Internet.

LaGuardia (1998) commented that, since the web has become a primary source for research and library resources, users are "set loose" to "grasp at what we may consider information straws" (p. S10). More than ever, the librarian's current role is to determine how patrons are utilizing the technologies and to point them towards the most relevant and authoritative information, whether through traditional in-person reference, virtual reference methods, or tools such as subject guides and tutorials.

Most libraries routinely collect reference statistics to measure the use of their reference services. An important question in libraries today is how changes in technology affect the numbers of reference questions. Few studies investigating the effect of technology on reference statistics are available versus a plethora of articles published in the 1990s and early 2000s. The authors present a review of the literature and examine reference statistics from the Reference and Information Services Department (RISD) at the University of North Texas (UNT) Libraries over a 16-year period. Gate counts and circulation data from 1997-2004 and 1998-2004, respectively, are also reviewed in order to determine if there are any relationships among these items and reference statistics.

LITERATURE REVIEW

Library Technology Changes

From the earliest online catalogs and integrated library systems, to the surge of CD-ROMs from the late 1980s to the mid-1990s, and finally to the widespread availability of the Internet, libraries are deeply affected by changes in technology. A survey by Oder (1996) reported that, between 1991-1996, academic libraries increased their spending on electronic resources by 90%, spending by special libraries increased 26%, and spending by public libraries averaged 16% yearly growth. The survey also indicated that academic and special libraries expected to curtail their CD-ROM purchases over the next three years.

In 1999, Bryant reported that public libraries increased their spending on web-based resources by 43% and expenditures by academic libraries rose 60% from 1996 figures. Surveyed libraries forecasted a 28% increase in web-based spending in 2000-2001.

An Association of Research Libraries (ARL) survey (2004) indicated that library expenditures as a percentage of university expenditures declined fairly rapidly from 1986-2001. Interestingly, expenditures in 1995 rose at a major clip, with smaller rises in 1997, 1998, and 2000, possibly due to the acquisition of online resources. Another ARL survey (Liu, 1999) reported that in 1996, 97% of the responding libraries created their first web site. Today, almost all academic libraries have some form of a web site, with the majority having a detailed and informative site that provides access to an extensive collection of electronic materials. More than 77% of public libraries in Canada and the United States have web sites as well (Prabha & Irwin, 2003).

Also, technology increased user expectations. The delivery of information and services is counted in hours, minutes, or seconds by our patrons rather than days or weeks, methods acceptable in the pre-web days. Leaving their home or office to come to the library for information needs is much less common than before and frequently viewed as an inconvenience (Irwin, 2004).

CD-ROMs

The advent of CD-ROMs in libraries generally had a positive effect on reference statistics. A survey of librarians across a spectrum of academic, special, and public libraries indicated that reference statistics rose 9% for in-person reference and 5% for telephone reference (Oder, 1996). Many librarians reported that questions about their remote services (dial-up databases and other electronic resources) accounted for the increase, with growth of 34% in these types of questions from 1995 to 1996. Tenopir and Ennis (2001) also reported that, in general, libraries' reference statistics decreased over the last decade or so, except for a small increase during the introduction of CD-ROMs.

The Internet

The Internet's impact on reference service occurred in many ways. Libraries once controlled access to CD-ROMs–users needed to come into the building or access the CD-ROMs through difficult remote methods. The web provided access to information, not just beyond library walls, but beyond the library's control (Howe, 2004). Users now had a choice about whether to use the library or the web to find information. Geng (2003) noted that the Internet affected reference in three major areas: human communication and interaction (the development of "virtual reference" and all the changes that have occurred), environment (reference interactions are now independent of place and time), and service expectations (librarians are still needed to help users find the required information but users have less recognition of this need for librarian intervention). Users are able to access resources at any time, excepting glitches, but most libraries only offer reference services during traditional working hours (Irwin, 2004). As well, the Internet requires the librarians and library users to have knowledge about both print and electronic sources of information (Straw, 2001). The provision of a mixture of online and print journals, for example, increased the complexity for the users.

Gate Counts and Circulation Statistics

A close correlation between reference counts and the number of people in the library is frequently noted by libraries (Novotny, 2002), and many libraries collect both sets of data. Albanese (2003) reported that gate counts began to increase in 2000 and are increasing steadily. Bertot et al. (2004) discovered that, between 2001 and 2003, some libraries reported an increase in gate counts and circulation statistics, but still experienced decreased reference statistics. He also reported that several libraries experienced an increase in reference statistics and suggested that the rise in numbers is traced to a realization by the users that the Internet does not have all the answers and the recognition that the library may have a purpose in today's society. Increased gate counts and other statistics may also be due, in part, to new libraries and/or enhanced user spaces. Baruth (2002) suggested that patrons will only use libraries if provided with what they need in an effective and satisfying manner. It is possible that the increases in gate counts and other usage statistics may herald similar changes in the number of reference questions.

Reference Statistics

Novotny (2002) noted that 78% of ARL libraries responding to a survey on reference service statistics reported that their reference transactions decreased in the last three years. Tenopir (2001) stated that, during a study of 40 academic librarians, 84% reported a decrease in the overall number of reference questions. Bertot (2004), Leahy (2003), and Bryant (1999) all reported declining reference counts. Cheng, Bischof, and Nathanson (2002) also reported a decline in reference desk statistics. Their usage statistics and user survey results indicated that students performed the majority of their research from dormitories or off-campus, and that faculty primarily accessed library resources from their offices or from their homes. The authors added that, in the fall of 2001, 38% of electronic journal usage occurred inside the library while 62% came from outside (Cheng et al., 2002), adding support to the premise that the provision of web-based resources is related to the decline in reference statistics. A recent faculty survey indicated that faculty members are continuing to request more and more electronic products (Jankowska, 2004). The increase in use from outside the library suggests that we need to reach users through such means as web-based tutorials and information-rich web pages. Jackson (2002) discussed the decline in reference statistics over the last 10 years and how various libraries are restructuring the reference function to accommodate the changing needs of the library patron.

Reference counts from virtual reference options are generally increasing. A study by Powell and Bradigan (2001) indicated that the e-mail reference question counts at the Prior Health Sciences Library at Ohio State University increased 209% between 1995 and 2000. Several academic librarians reported an increase in telephone reference (Tenopir, 2001). Questions received by the Internet Public Library (IPL) steadily increased (Mon, 2000). In 1995, the IPL responded to 1,116 questions and in 1999 answered 7,054 queries, an increase of 532%. Murray and Tschernitz (2004) reported, however, that the Victorian Information Service Network, an Australian virtual reference consortium for public libraries, experienced decreasing statistics since its inception in 1994. The authors noted that the majority of the 65 librarians surveyed reported a decline in reference questions of 15.5% annually; however, 12 (18%) of the librarians noted an increase of 17% per annum. The authors added that reference statistics rose 1.6% across Victorian public libraries since 1996. The Division of Library and Information Services in Florida reported an increase in queries from 17,508 in 1997/1998 to 30,314 in 2001/2002, a growth of 73% (Murray & Tschernitz, 2004). This rise is attributed to the development of a new web portal and the establishment of an e-mail reference service. These results lend credence to the premise that virtual reference services are, in general, experiencing an increase in the number of questions received.

Effects on the Reference Desk

Several authors noted that, despite a decline in reference statistics, reference librarians are as busy as ever. Bertot et al. (2004) noted that some librarians reported a decrease in reference, circulation and gate counts, but also stated that the reference staff is just as busy or busier when statistics decreased due to questions being more intricate. Summey (1997) and Tenopir (2001) found similar results. Leahy (2003) suggested that the questions asked at the typical reference desk are fewer but much more complex, resulting in librarians spending more time on each question. The heightened expectation that everything is available online increased the length and complexity of reference questions. For example, library patrons *expect* to find in-depth information about a company rather than just an address (Tenopir & Ennis, 2001).

Few published studies reported on the duration of reference questions. Spencer and Dorsey (1998) examined the time taken by Arizona State University librarians to answer reference questions. The authors noted that librarians answered 72.1% of the questions in 1-5 minutes, 18.4% in 6-10 minutes, and 9% in 11 minutes or more. While this study does not offer a historical perspective and may be a little outdated given the pace of technology, the data does provide a starting point for further studies. Novotney (2002) reported that, at the University of California at Irvine, reference questions averaged approximately 7 minutes.

Despite the fact that today's library users are, in general, more familiar with Internet and computer technologies, the complexity and length of time needed to answer questions appears to be increasing. Much of the increase may be due to the need for instruction on information literacy and search concepts. Rather than approaching the reference desk first, patrons frequently ask for reference assistance only after they attempt to search for information on their own and fail to find anything after a significant period of time (Flanagan & Horowitz, 2000). Reference staff must repeat the steps the patron performed, as well as find new avenues to locate the appropriate answer. Murray and Tschernitz (2004) reported the results of a survey of librarians that suggested the number of directional or quick questions and the number of more complicated questions increased, while the number of medium length questions decreased. Warner (2001) noted that gathering information on what types of questions were asked would be helpful in determining the level of reference desk activity. Michael Gorman recently suggested that another reason for declining reference statistics may be the proliferation of information on library web pages (Albanese, 2003). Many of the basic questions, such as hours, collections, locations, and tutorials, can be found using these pages. Gorman hypothesized that if we only analyzed the numbers of in-depth questions, the decline would not be as noticeable.

What To Do?

A review of the literature suggests that reference questions are taking longer to answer and are more extensive, yet the actual number of questions is declining. Reference managers may need to reconsider how reference services are measured. Statistics may be lower due to issues with the traditional recording method of "one patron, one tick." Today's busy reference desk with more time-intensive questions is not well represented using this system (Warner, 2001). Frequently, the librarians guide the patron through several steps, including database searching, catalog use, and printing or photocopying procedures. The time spent is not obvious with the "one tick" method since the librarian answered at least three questions, and probably more, when discussions about keywords, Boolean operators, and search strategies are taken into account. Summey (1997) expressed concern that the teaching function is increasing at the reference desk and that the staff is under greater pressure to remain ahead of technology changes without having sufficient training.

Traditional statistical recording systems also may not include reference questions answered beyond the reference desk. Tenopir (1998) suggested that librarians are spending more time in the academic departments and we should consider whether these types of questions are being recorded in the statistics. The reliance on e-mail as a form of communication likely reduced statistics as the questions asked in e-mail are not usually counted in the reference statistics.

Bertot et al. (2004) stated that library managers need to examine the trends in reference statistics and determine which services and resources the patrons actually use. The economics of reference services should be studied as well (Lankes, Gross, & McClure, 2003). However, to first determine the costs, an effective method of reference statistic keeping must be developed. Warner (2001) discussed a revised method of recording reference statistics that divides the questions into four categories: non-resource based, skill-based, strategy-based, and consultation.

Seven reference staff members preferred using the new method, two had no preference, and one preferred the old way. One participant stated that the new system accurately described the services provided. The development of a recording system that more closely represents what the reference staff actually does will assist in determining the most effective means of providing services (Lankes et al., 2003). In addition, an effective method of recording reference transactions provides documentation to aid in acquiring the support needed to offer desired services.

The Use of Statistics

Cheng et al. (2002) warned readers that statistics gathering can become an all consuming process, yet the effective evaluation of the statistics and how they can improve services may not always take priority. The authors exhorted librarians to focus on gathering statistics that can be used to improve services. Statistics should provide useful information on the changes in usage patterns and user behaviors. Banks (1999) noted that libraries need to be aware of how patrons are actually using the services and what user needs are not being met.

Tenopir and Ennis (1998) suggested that the quality of the answers should be measured. Bravy and Feather (2001) discussed the importance of libraries finding qualitative measures for services as well as effective quantifiable statistics. These articles remind librarians that the heart of reference service is about quality rather than quantity.

Bravy and Feather (2001) stated that few studies quantitatively addressed the impact of technology on libraries. They noted that this is usually because it is difficult to determine a causal relationship among variables. One study that does report on the correlations among variables is Banks (1999), who found a positive relationship between reduced gate count numbers and reduced circulation, reference, and online catalog search statistics.

Why Are Reference Statistics Decreasing?

Many of the articles discussed the possible influences on the decline of reference desk statistics. Major trends in the suggestions are the users' assumed familiarity with Internet searching and the growth of distance education courses, allowing students to use their local libraries rather than the library of the school offering the course or degree. The reticence of users to admit that they need help may also contribute to the decline, especially as many users feel that web-based products should be as easy to use as their favorite search engine and become easily frustrated when this is not true. Novotny (2002) reported that comments received by ARL members suggested that online resources are, in part, contributing to the decline in reference questions. Murray and Tschernitz (2004) noted that competition from online information vendors, such as Ask Jeeves and Information Please, may be reducing reference statistics. Collaborative systems, such as the Internet Public Library, may also be answering "our" reference questions since patrons are becoming more used to searching the web than contacting their local librarian. Many corporations and government agencies have e-mail or chat reference options available, and this may reduce the need to contact local libraries as well.

OVERVIEW OF UNT AND THE LIBRARIES

The University

The University of North Texas is primarily a commuter campus located in Denton, Texas, near Dallas and Fort Worth. Within the last several years, UNT developed into a system that now includes campuses in Dallas and Fort Worth. There are 98 bachelor, 128 masters, and 48 doctoral programs, with approximately 7,000 faculty and staff. While known for such programs as music, education, and library and information science, UNT includes a variety of high-quality programs across the humanities, social sciences, and sciences.

Growth in student numbers is a dominant force at UNT. While there were only 24,500 students enrolled in 1988, there are now more than 37,000. Annual course enrollment data from 1994 to 2004 is shown in Table 1, displaying the total number of students enrolled in all courses offered in a given year. It shows that undergraduate enrollment experienced the largest increase. While doctoral study enrollments remained relatively constant, enrollment in post-bachelors and masters programs increased slightly over the years, although the increase is not consistent.

UNT emphasized online education using WebCT during recent years. In 2003, 9,155 students enrolled in web-based distance education courses compared to 266 enrolled in the spring semester of 1998, the

TABLE 1. Total Course Enrollment from 1994-2004

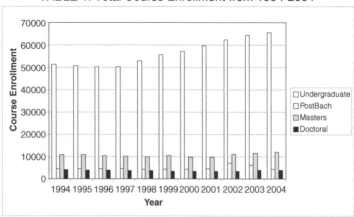

first time UNT offered online courses. The School of Library and Information Science is a major contributor to the online learning environment, with many courses offered entirely online.

The Libraries

The UNT Libraries include the A.M. Willis Library, which houses the general reference, music, humanities and social sciences collections, government documents, digital projects, a rare book collection and archives; the Science and Technology Library, which supports the "hard" sciences, as well as psychology and behavior sciences; the Media Library and the Multimedia Development Lab, which specialize in audio-visual materials, computer software, and web design for academic departments; the Research Park Library, created in 2004 to support the newly-established College of Engineering; and the Annex, which houses the Technical Services and Preservations units. Additional information on the UNT Libraries can be found at www.library.unt.edu.

This article is limited to discussion of statistics from the Reference and Information Services unit, which includes the general reference desk in the Willis Library, and the science and technology reference desk. Staff at these locations also monitor the toll-free reference number, e-mail reference system, and online chat service.

Expenditures and Numbers for Electronic Resources in the Libraries

The UNT Libraries ventured into the electronic revolution with the online public access catalog in 1983. By 1992, the Libraries offered several stand alone databases provided by SilverPlatter. Between 1992 and 1994, the emphasis shifted to acquiring electronic resources, resulting in expenditures for the 1995/1996 fiscal year of $268,220 for CD-ROMs and $8,200 for other electronic products. In March 1998, the Libraries provided users with more than 500 electronic resources, many of these being CD-ROMs. By March 2000, CD-ROMs, including more than 300 e-journals, comprised 90% of the total electronic resources.

In the summer of 2000, the Libraries replaced CD-ROMs with web-based resources. The Libraries' LAN department created an in-house system to network resources and provided remote access to the CD-ROMs using Citrix (a "helper" program). With the increasing prominence of Internet-based products, the Libraries agreed to convert

CD-ROM products to the web in order to provide more efficient access for the patrons and fewer challenges for the LAN department. In February 2001, users had access to over 700 resources on CD-ROM. By May 2002, only 25 resources remained on CD-ROM, with the rest of the resources available over the web. Fiscal year 2002/2003 saw expenditures of $86,296 for CD-ROMs, with the majority of the dollars going towards SciFinder Scholar and the Science Citation Indexes, and $2.04 million for web-based resources. Currently, there are over 256 web-based databases and indexes and over 3,700 e-journals.

METHODS AND MATERIALS

This article investigates how reference statistics are affected by technology using data from 1989-2004. Statistics are compiled from the Reference and Information Services Department (RISD), which underwent several transformations during the period under review. Prior to 1988 and until December 2000, the Science and Technology Reference Department (SciTech) operated as a separate entity from the Willis Library Reference Department (Willis). Since we wanted to investigate any relationships between the sciences and the social sciences/humanities, the SciTech statistics are included in the analysis. In 1996, the collection of statistics become voluntary for library departments; the Science and Technology Reference Department did not gather usage statistics until its merger with the Willis Library Reference Department in late 2000.

Physical reference desks are maintained in both libraries. Reference questions are categorized as "directional" and "reference," and these are combined for the purposes of this article. The UNT Libraries also support a toll-free telephone number. Phone calls are logged as regular statistics. In September 1997, the Libraries introduced an Ask-A-Librarian e-mail reference service and continues still. In May 1999, the Libraries introduced the basic chat reference service, named the "Online Reference Help Desk," which continued until its upgrade to the Docutek software in May 2004. The switch to Docutek provided us with a highly desired co-browsing environment.

Beginning in January 1989, we entered monthly reference statistics into an Excel spreadsheet and analyzed them by calendar year. Service points not completing statistics for a full year are eliminated from the calculations for that particular year. Yearly statistics are displayed using bar graphs.

Gate counts from the Willis Library and the SciTech library during 1997-2004 are also examined to investigate if there is a relationship between the counts and the reference statistics, and whether the results are different between the two reference desks. Circulation figures from 1998-2004 are also provided to determine if these have a relationship with reference statistics.

RESULTS

Gate counts for 1997-2004 are shown in Table 2. Willis gate counts increased overall, although they fluctuate by year. The statistics increased more than 260,000, or 39%. SciTech's gate counts are on a slow downturn, with a drop of 74,000, or 24%. Total gate counts increased by approximately 188,000, or 19%.

The circulation statistics from 1998 to 2004 are shown in Table 3. Both Willis and SciTech circulation counts experienced a bowl-shaped effect. Willis counts dropped by 20,000 overall resulting in an 11% decrease, but began to increase in 2003 and dramatically increased in 2004 by 16,000 (11%). SciTech experienced an overall decrease of 11,000 or 17%, yet increased by more than 5,000 (11%) between 2003 and 2004.

Table 4 presents the trends in annual reference statistics from 1989 until 2004. The largest bar is the total of all service points, with the

TABLE 2. Gate Counts from 1997-2004

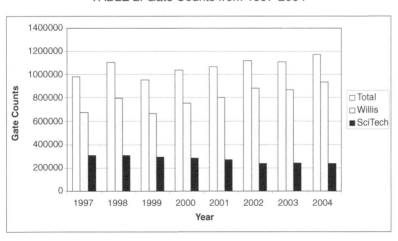

TABLE 3. Circulation Costs from 1998-2004

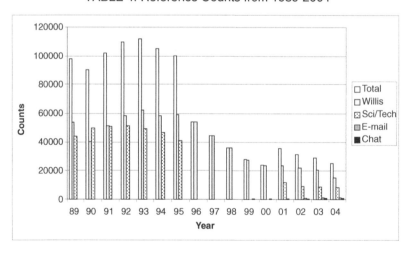

TABLE 4. Reference Counts from 1989-2004

next largest (usually) being Willis, then SciTech. There is a trend of rising counts between 1991 and 1993, most likely due to the increase in CD-ROM products. As noted in the *Methods and Materials* section, statistics from SciTech are not available from 1996-2000. The e-mail service began in 1999 and contributed a small amount to the totals. The

Libraries initiated chat reference in 2000. Both forms of virtual reference are graphed in Tables 6 and 7 and allows for a full analysis of their counts.

Table 5 breaks out the reference data from 1989 to 1995 to clearly illustrate the trends for these years. It is noteworthy that the trends are not consistent between the two desks. SciTech counts rose to a high in 1990 and stayed relatively constant until decreasing in 1994. Willis counts experienced a noticeable decline in 1990 then rose until 1993.

The trends in reference question counts from 1996-2004 are shown in Table 6. From 1996 to 2000, the values for the Total and Willis are approximately the same, since counts for SciTech were not being collected during this period. The small differences between the Total and Willis are due to counts from the e-mail and chat services. Between 1996 and 2000, Willis counts experienced a rapid decline, likely due to users becoming more accustomed to CD-ROM technology, resulting in fewer questions at the reference desks.

In December 2000, the Science and Technology Reference Department merged with the Willis Reference Department and question counts for SciTech began to be recorded in January 2001. Numbers of questions asked at both reference desks are decreasing at approximately the same rate. SciTech counts decreased by 3,300 counts, or 29%, from 2001 to 2004, while Willis counts decreased by 8,300, or 35%. How-

TABLE 5. Reference Statistics from 1989-1995

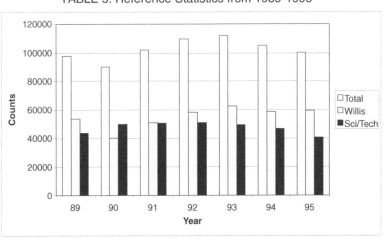

TABLE 6. Reference Counts from 1996-2004

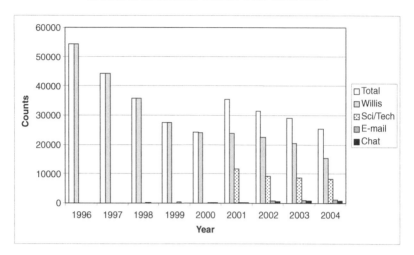

ever, Willis experienced a substantial drop from 2003-2004, decreasing by nearly 5,000, or 25%.

Table 7 provides the annual statistics for the e-mail and chat services. E-mail service started in September of 1997; the Libraries initiated the chat system in May 1999. Since the numbers are displayed on an annual basis, only full years are included as previously noted. As expected, the statistics for both services are on the rise, although each initially experienced a small decrease.

ANALYSIS

In recent years, library instruction and tours increased tremendously. Beginning in 2000, students enrolled in Introductory English are required to attend training sessions, providing a large increase in gate counts for Willis, compared to 1999. A variety of other classes are brought into the Libraries for instruction. In the fall of 2004, an Introductory Communications course also required mandatory instruction. This increase primarily affected Willis gate counts (Table 2) as the library houses the instruction rooms. In addition, the establishment of a coffee bar in Willis, the "CyberCafe," may have increased foot traffic.

TABLE 7. E-mail and Chat Counts from 1998-2004

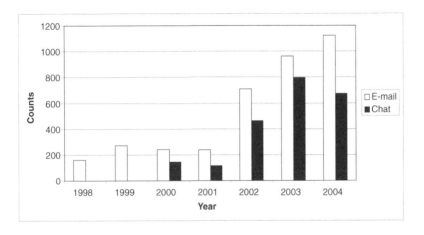

Increased student enrollment also contributed to the rise in Willis gate counts.

The decrease in SciTech's gate counts (Table 2) may be due to several factors. Remote access to the Libraries' resources already took place by 1998. The Libraries actively pursued online journals beginning in 2000, and accessed to the major science packages (ScienceDirect, Blackwell Synergy, Springer Link, and Wiley) by 2002. As a majority of SciTech's foot traffic is traditionally journal-related, the move to online journals contributed to the reduced gate counts. Since September 11, 2001, UNT, like most universities, experienced increased difficulties with obtaining foreign graduate students. Graduate students comprised a high percentage of SciTech's foot traffic and the reduction in numbers affected gate counts. Based on all these factors, we can conclude that access to library resources without coming into the libraries and changes in the composition of the users affected gate counts.

Possible reasons for the increases in circulation figures (Table 3) are improved communication between the liaison librarians and the departments to advertise the "new acquisitions" web page and the effects of increased library instruction, both of which help users find relevant items. The online catalog's user interface received a face-lift in early 2004, which may have increased the use of the catalog and thus provided more effective access to the circulating collection.

Tenopir and Ennis (2001) reported that a survey of 40 librarians indicated that the use of CD-ROMs in libraries resulted in increased numbers of reference statistics. The increased counts occurred anywhere from the mid to late 1980s up to the early 1990s, depending on when the libraries adopted CD-ROM technology. UNT Libraries first installed science-based CD-ROMs, hence, as noted in Tables 4 and 5, the initial rise in SciTech reference counts in 1990 and continuing until 1993, versus the rise in Willis counts beginning in 1991 and retaining an overall increase until 1995. The sustained increase in reference counts during these years may be due to the learning curve for users or the time taken for CD-ROMs to become publicly available outside of libraries. Also, SciTech surpassed Willis reference counts in 1990, the first year the Science Library introduced CD-ROMs. This supports the hypothesis that the introduction of CD-ROMs increased reference counts.

If the 2004 counts are removed in Table 6, SciTech experienced a decrease of 26% between 2001 and 2003, while Willis counts decreased by only 13%. It is also interesting to note that the majority of SciTech's decrease occurred between 2001 and 2002 (29%) and tapered off in the subsequent two years. A possible explanation for this is that more of the science-related resources became available online before the social sciences and humanities items, and by 2002, users' familiarity with the Internet substantially increased. In addition, science disciplines tend to rely more on collegial interactions than library reference services (Hirsh, 2001; Hertzum & Pejtersen, 2000; Leckie et al., 1996). Another factor potentially influencing the decline in SciTech recently is the impact of September 11, 2001 on the ability of educational institutions to recruit foreign graduate students. These students are a primary user group of the SciTech Reference Desk.

The drop in 2004 counts for Willis library may be a result of the increase in library instruction, more effective promotion of our subject and class pages, increased use of the virtual reference system, or a combination of the above.

In Table 7, the increase in questions from virtual reference options results in a rise of 602% (900 questions) from 1998 to 2004 for e-mail, and 370% (528 questions) for chat from its inception until 2004. Murray and Tschernitz (2004), Powell and Bradigan (2001), and Mon (2000) reported an increase in reference statistics as noted in the literature review. These results, along with the data from the UNT Libraries' chat and e-mail services, lend credence to the premise that the Libraries' remote reference services are, for the most part, experiencing an increase in the number of questions asked.

Due to the decrease in chat questions in 2004, we examined the data in Table 7 more closely. Chat counts reduced by 125 questions, or 16%, while e-mail counts increased by 163, or 17%. In the spring of 2004, the chat moved from a basic text system to Docutek's co-browsing software, which we thought more attractive and effective for our users. The decline in chat statistics is likely due to initial problems with the software, reduced advertising while we adjusted to the new software, and recent problems with the software when we determined that the Service Pack 2 (SP2) upgrade for Microsoft XP "broke" the co-browsing ability, rather than users not preferring the new software. When Docutek produces a patch for SP2 problem, advertising the chat reference service will resume and expect an increase in usage of the system.

Despite an overwhelming increase in chat and e-mail statistics, they are not counter-acting the decrease in face-to-face reference. One librarian reported that, while her library's in-person queries decreased, the overall volume remained similar due to the rise in statistics from other forms of reference service. However, most libraries are not seeing virtual reference statistics compensate for the decrease in traditional reference statistics (Tenopir, 2001).

As indicated earlier, SciTech reference question counts dropped substantially between 2001 and 2003 when web-based resources replaced many CD-ROM products and allowed the web resources to be remotely accessible in a seamless manner. Since more and more use of library resources are occurring from outside the library, we need to reach users through web-based means, such as online tutorials and specially created subject guides and class pages.

From the literature review, we noticed that several authors suggested that, although reference statistics are declining, the reference staff is as busy as they used to be (Bertot et al., 2004; Tenopir, 2001; and Summey, 1997). Leahy (2003) suggested that the complexity of the questions is increasing; thus, the average time required to answer questions is likewise increasing. The study by Spencer and Dorsey (1998) provides a starting point for examining the time necessary to answer reference questions.

Anecdotal data from both reference desks support the idea that questions are frequently more complex and require a variety of steps; hence, the time taken to successfully answer the questions may be longer than before the CD-ROM and Internet technology. One online area that users have difficulty with is using our online catalog. Users may need to search through several entries to find what they need. There are also an increasing number of technically-oriented questions, especially concerning remote access problems, the majority of which require assistance from our LAN department or from the University's Academic Computing Services. The assumption that all information is online contributes to the length and intensity of reference questions (Leahy, 2003) as patrons want the librarians to search every possible avenue, and even then the patrons seem to think that we are not doing our jobs effectively if we are unable to locate exactly what they need.

The literature review indicated that several authors are concerned that the "usual" way of recording statistics, "the one question, one tick method," is not representing the work performed at the reference desk or capturing the real work of today's reference librarians. The UNT Libraries is advocating the creation and use of tutorials, subject pages, and class-specific pages, and we already have a good variety of these available. Given that the majority of today's users seek online resources before approaching libraries, a well-designed, informative and useable web page may be answering many questions without intervention. It is possible that we should, as Gorman suggests, add these web page hits to our reference counts.

Traditional statistical recording systems also may not include reference questions that are answered beyond the reference desk. Tenopir (1998) suggested that librarians are spending more time in the academic departments and we should consider whether these types of questions are being recorded in the statistics. Reference librarians at UNT Libraries have liaison duties and frequently do not record liaison-related transactions, such as e-mail queries.

The increase in online courses could also be reducing the reference statistics. Since UNT's enrollment in online courses increased 97% between 1998 and 2004, corresponding to a 28% decrease in reference questions during the same years, one could logically assume a relationship. Although UNT offers e-mail and an interactive virtual reference options, as well as a toll-free number, it is possible that students studying online may prefer to use their local libraries for assistance. Improved resource provision, such as electronic reserves for online courses, may also reduce the number of questions from online learners.

CONCLUSIONS AND FUTURE RESEARCH

The results of the analyses provide fruitful information for the continued discussion of the effect of technology on reference question statistics. Both reference desks experienced reduced in-person reference counts over the years examined. Willis and SciTech both experienced an increase in reference statistics during the CD-ROM era. Web-based products resulted in small increases in Willis reference stats in 2001. Overall, however, the Internet appeared to have little effect on reference statistics except perhaps to slow the rate of the decrease. The e-mail and chat services are increasing substantially, with e-mail growing at a more rapid rate. This result adds to the growing literature supporting the idea that technological changes do affect reference question statistics.

Although Willis gate counts are increasing, the statistics decreased when the reduction in SciTech figures are included. The introduction of web-based materials may have contributed to the rise in Willis gate counts, as this corresponds to a lower rate of decline in reference questions as well. Circulation counts are increasing slowly. Since the UNT Libraries are experiencing some increases in gate counts, circulation figures, and virtual reference counts, the in-person reference question numbers may also increase or at least experience a reduced rate of decline in the future.

In a follow-up paper, the authors plan on taking a formal statistical approach, such as examining the significance and relationship among the different variables that may affect reference statistics, including the growth of distance education courses, gate counts, discipline differences, and related issues. The contributions of tutorials, subject guides, and class pages to reference services would also be beneficial to know. Reference services must determine more accurate means to collect statistics that reflect the actual use of the services. The statistics should include online reference methods and possibly web page statistics as the proliferation of library-based web pages may indeed, as Gorman suggested, be answering many of the questions that face-to-face reference services answered in the past. Knowing what questions our users are asking, regardless of venue, and knowing how they are using the resources we provide through our reference web pages, would assist us in providing needed services and collections in a proactive manner.

REFERENCES

Albanese, A. R. (2003). Deserted no more. *Library Journal, 128*(7), 34-36.

Association of Research Libraries (2004). *Library expenditures as a percent of University expenditures 1996-2001.* Retrieved October 23, 2004, from http://www.arl. org/stats/eg/graph17.html.

Banks, J. (1999). Does building traffic affect circulation, OPAC searching, or reference desk activity? *Library Computing, 18*(4), 327-333.

Baruth, B. (2002). Missing pieces that fill in the academic library puzzle. *American Libraries, 33*(6), 58-63.

Bertot, J. C., McClure, C. R., Davis, D. M., & Ryan, J. (2004). Capture usage with e-metrics. *Library Journal, 129*(8), 30-32.

Bravy, G. J., & Feather, K. C. (2001). The impact of electronic access on basic library services: One academic law library's experience. *Law Library Journal, 93*(2), 261-268.

Bryant, E. (1999). Triumph of the web. *Library Journal, 124*(19), 4-6.

Cheng, R., Bischof, S., & Nathanson, A. J. (2002). Data collection for user-oriented library services: Wesleyan University Library's experience. *OCLC Systems & Services, 18*(4), 195-204.

Flanagan, P., & Horowitz, L. R. (2000). Exploring new service models: Can consolidating public service points improve response to customer needs? *The Journal of Academic Librarianship, 26*(5), 329-339.

Geng, T. H. (2003). The impact of Internet on library reference service. Consal, Research Centre, Topical Briefs. Retrieved February 5, 2005, from www.consal.org. sg/resource/brief/default.asp?page=7.

Gromov, G. (2002). *The roads and crossroads of Internet history: Growth of the Internet.* Retrieved December 5, 2005, from History of the Internet and WWW Web site: http://www.netvalley.com/intvalstat.html.

Hertzum, M., & Pejtersen, A. M. (2000). The information-seeking practices of engineers: Searching for documents as well as for people. *Information Processing & Management, 36*(5), 761-778.

Hirsh, S. G. (2000). Information needs, information seeking, and communication in an industrial R & D environment. *Proceedings of the 63rd Annual Meeting of the American Society for Information Science, 37*, 473-486.

Howe, W. (2004). *A brief history of the Internet.* Retrieved December 16, 2005, from http://www.walthowe.com/navnet/history.html.

Irwin, R. D. (2004). Emerging issues in library web collections. *Libres: Library and Information Science Research Electronic Journal, 14*(1). Retrieved November 6, 2005, from http://libres.curtin.edu.au/libres14n1/March%2004_Ess&Op_IrwinDec4_03final.htm.

Jackson, R. (2002). Revolution or evolution: Reference planning in ARL libraries. *Reference Services Review, 30*(3), 212-228.

Jankowska, M. A. (2004). Identifying university professors' information needs in the challenging environment of information and communication technologies. *The Journal of Academic Librarianship, 30*(1), 51-66.

LaGuardia, C. (1998). Online links: Users' needs, librarians' roles. *Library Journal, Reference Supplement, 123*(19), S10-S11.

Lankes, D., Gross, M., & McClure, C. R. (2003). Costs, statistics, measures, and standards for digital reference services: A preliminary view. *Library Trends, 51*(3), 401-413.

Leahy, L. (2003). Managing an academic reference department. *The Reference Librarian, 81*, 5-15.

Leckie, G. J., Pettigrew, K. E., & Sylvain, C. (1996). Modeling the information seeking of professionals: A general model derived from research on engineers, health care professionals, and lawyers. *The Library Quarterly, 66*(2), 161-193.

Liu, Y. P. (1999). *Web page development and management.* ARL Spec Kit 246. Association of Research Libraries: Washington, D.C.

Mon, L. (2000). Digital reference service. *Government Information Quarterly, 17*(3), 309-318.

Murray, J., & Tschernitz, C. (2004). The Internet myth: Emerging trends in reference enquiries. *Aplis, 17*(2), 80-88.

Novotny, E. (2002). *Reference service statistics and assessment.* ARL Spec Kit 268. Association of Research Libraries: Washington, D.C.

Oder, N. (1996). Online resources emerge. *Library Journal,* Reference Supplement, *121*(19), S74-S76.

Powell, C. A., & Bradigan, P. S. (2001). E-mail reference service: Characteristics and effects on overall references at an academic health sciences library. *Reference & User Services Quarterly, 41*(2), 170-178.

Prabha, C., & Irwin, R. (2003). Web technology in public libraries: Findings from research. *Library Hi Tech, 21*(1), 62-69.

Spencer, J. S., & Dorsey, L. (1998). Assessing time spent on reference questions at an urban university library. *The Journal of Academic Librarianship, 24*(4), 290-294.

Straw, J. E. (2001). From magicians to teachers: The development of electronic reference in libraries: 1930-2000. *The Reference Librarian,* 74, 1-12.

Summey, T. P. (1997). Techno reference: Impact of electronic reference resources on traditional reference services. *The Reference Librarian,* 59, 103-111.

Tenopir, C. (1998). Reference use statistics. *Library Journal, 123*(8), 32-34.

Tenopir, C. (2001). Virtual reference services in a real world. *Library Journal, 126*(12), 38-40.

Tenopir, C., & Ennis, L. (1998). The impact of digital reference on librarians and library users. *Online, 22*(6), 84-6, 88.

Tenopir, C., & Ennis, L. (2001). Reference services in the new millennium. *Online, 25*(4), 40-42, 44-45.

Warner, D. G. (2001). A new classification for reference statistics. *Reference & User Services Quarterly, 41*(1), 51-55.

Staffing Needs of the Reference Desk at the University of Tennessee at Chattanooga: A Statistical Approach

Sarla R. Murgai

SUMMARY. This study grew out of a need to assess reference desk data and determine two items: the number of questions handled for the last three years and the times when the desk should be double staffed. Analysis of the data by chi-square standardized residuals identified the days of the week, and the times during the day of heavy and light use. Data sort identified the heavy/light use weeks, months, and semesters. Descriptive analysis also established the variability and the range of data. When comparing data from week to week for the random sample years with the data collected by every hour for every day of the week for the non-random sample years, this revealed a very similar pattern. Heavy days, weeks, hours, and months fell into a similar pattern from semester to semester and from year to year. Other academic libraries can follow this model and apply it to their work environment after adjusting for their academic calendar and user behavior. *[Article copies available for a fee from The Haworth Document Delivery Service: 1-800-HAWORTH. E-mail address: <docdelivery@haworthpress.com> Website: <http://www.HaworthPress.com> © 2006 by The Haworth Press, Inc. All rights reserved.]*

Sarla R. Murgai is Associate Professor and Reference Librarian, University of Tennessee at Chattanooga, Chattanooga, TN 37403 (E-mail: Sarla-murgai@utc.edu).

[Haworth co-indexing entry note]: "Staffing Needs of the Reference Desk at the University of Tennessee at Chattanooga: A Statistical Approach." Murgai, Sarla R. Co-published simultaneously in *Public Services Quarterly* (The Haworth Information Press, an imprint of The Haworth Press, Inc.) Vol. 2, No. 2/3, 2006, pp. 167-190; and: *Reference Assessment and Evaluation* (ed: Tom Diamond, and Mark Sanders) The Haworth Information Press, an imprint of The Haworth Press, Inc., 2006, pp. 167-190. Single or multiple copies of this article are available for a fee from The Haworth Document Delivery Service [1-800-HAWORTH, 9:00 a.m. - 5:00 p.m. (EST). E-mail address: docdelivery@haworthpress.com].

Available online at http://www.haworthpress.com/web/PSQ
© 2006 by The Haworth Press, Inc. All rights reserved.
doi:10.1300/J295v02n02_11

KEYWORDS. Reference desk staffing, statistics, transaction counts

INTRODUCTION

Reference service is quintessentially a human science. It is based on personal relationships between the librarians and patrons (Richardson, 2002, p. 42). Automation has lent some efficiency and ease to the process, however, it has not reduced the need for human help (Rettig, 2004). Web-based reference services may have the potential to improve the efficiency and productivity of reference service. But in order to realize that potential, we have to find better methods to measure the entire reference process. That includes the total number of reference questions, types of reference questions, the number of reference personnel, and the time librarians spend answering reference questions. Libraries also need to estimate the costs of equipment, networks, and communication structure.

Today is an age of accountability. There is a need to measure the managerial effectiveness of reference and optimize the services. Information and reference services are now a commodity that is for sale in the marketplace. Librarians are in competition with the database aggregators and suppliers and need to deliver these services more efficiently (Glockner, 2004; Rettig, 2004; Blandy, Martin, and Strife, eds., 1992; Summerhill, 1994; Murgai, 1986). It is very important to understand and document how demand, workload, and accessibility are interrelated. Even though there is no perfect way to determine how busy reference is going to be at any given moment, statistics can paint a picture of busy versus slow service times. These data can help predict future demand (Taylor, 1994). This paper is an attempt to statistically analyze transaction counts at the reference desk of the Lupton Library of The University of Tennessee at Chattanooga (UTC) and determine the appropriate level of staffing needed at the reference desk.

LITERATURE REVIEW

Now that libraries are enjoying the advantages of automated online catalogs, acquisitions, circulation, databases, and the Internet, it is time to evaluate the efficiency and effectiveness of reference services. Costs are high since most of the reference services are provided in-person by a professional librarian. Kuhlman (1995) assessed these costs to be 20%

of the budget for a selection of universities and college libraries. The Lupton Library Reference department's 2004-2005 budget for including salaries (faculty and student assistants) and materials equaled 35% of the total library budget. This is one and a half times Kuhlman's 1995 estimate of 20%. To compound these matters, most university libraries have experienced drastic budget cuts in recent years. Campus demands have led to increased acquisition of electronic resources, while the prices for serials skyrocket. In light of all these changes, there is definitely a need to reassess the effectiveness of staff's productivity to justify the costs of reference (Glockner, 2004; Coffman and Saxton, 1999; Summerhill, 1994; Cummins, 1992). Most of the authors emphasize the importance of establishing quantitative and qualitative standards for reference services. They urge librarians to evaluate the services within the framework of a continually changing environment (print vs. electronic), and the continuing problem of library resource reduction (Glockner, 2004; Bundt, 2000; Blandy, Martin, & Strife, 1992). Statistical analysis methods are considered logical, objective, and reliable for data collection and for establishing standards for evaluating reference service. A review of the reference statistical literature shows that, since the 1980s and 1990s, many major university libraries explored the feasibility of using the random sampling method for collecting reference use data and adopted that method for gathering data and statistically analyzing the reference use at their institutions (Lochstet and Lehman, 1999; Dennison, 1999; Schlesinger, 1997; Maxstadt, 1988; Witucke and Schumaker, 1991; Kessellman and Watstein, 1987; Kantor, 1984).

In these studies, the collection and analysis of use data occurs from various aspects in which reference services is delivered: by the patron type (faculty, students, and others), by subject, and by number of questions asked at the reference desk. Measures used to record and evaluate reference questions include directional or research questions, the time taken to answer a question, resources used to answer a question, staff hours involved, questions answered through e-mail, time spent on coaching/consultation, and number of virtual reference questions.

Reference service departments are making some progress in quantifying the amount and quality of services rendered. Also, they gained important insights into the complexity of reference service. As Rettig (2004, p. 6) recently stated, "Complexity of information resources combined with complexity of the systems used to organize library resources indicates that a knowledgeable human should be available to answer reference questions." Desk-centered statistics are just one piece of a larger puzzle of accounting for all modes of library service. Libraries are also challenged to allocate personnel to chat and e-mail reference. A well-trained paraprofessional may be able to help with simple directional questions, but one can never predict when a simple reference question will transform into a complex reference question. Reference librarians need to staff the desk at all times.

Felix Chu (1997) writes that staffing the reference desk by paraprofessionals would be a step backwards. On college campuses, parents, students, and legislators want full-time faculty to teach. In this sense, librarians are akin to full-time professors who have the breadth of knowledge necessary to participate in the process of giving quality education to students. In such an atmosphere, Chu feels "there is a need to rethink whether a seemingly fiscally prudent move on our part to staff the reference desk with students and graduate assistants or clerical staff may be viewed as library's abdication of its role in providing quality education for students" (p. 713).

According to Thompson R. Cummins (1992), staffing involves an equitable distribution of existing or reduced personnel to meet the identified workload. Understaffing can impact the quality of service delivered as much as overstaffing can waste valuable time and personnel resources (p. 158). Cummins suggests that librarians evaluate the effectiveness of the staff's productivity by creating specific configurations. He proposes a formula based on the total number of reference questions answered per staff and the average time required for answering each question. Accordingly, such calculations help in developing an assignment pattern to make sure that there are enough staff available to meet the need during the hours and days the library is open.

Aaron Schlesinger (1997) conducted research to find out if the information desk needed staffing changes. He calculated an average number of questions asked at the information desk by the hour and the week as well as total man-hours. Results indicated that extra staff would be needed on Tuesdays, Wednesdays, Saturdays, and Sundays. Mondays are already assigned the most hours for they tended to be the busiest day of the week. Over 60% of all the questions asked during his study are reference questions, each taking an average of six minutes to answer. Directional questions accounted for about 19% of the questions.

BACKGROUND

The average annual enrollment at UTC is around 9,000. UTC's Lupton Library maintains a collection of over 496,000 books, 1,800 current periodical subscriptions, 25,000 reels of microfilm, and provides access to the online catalog and about one hundred databases. Professional librarians staff the reference desk from 7:50 a.m. to 10 p.m., Monday through Thursday. On Friday, the desk is staffed till 5 p.m. On Saturday, the desk is staffed from 10 a.m. to 4 p.m. and on Sunday from 2 p.m. to 10 p.m. At times during the fall and the spring semesters, double staffing is required to handle patrons' questions and also to provide phone backup service. Similarly, during summer and semester breaks when the patron load decreases, librarians emphasize other activities like collection development, collection maintenance, weeding, preparation of handouts, and planning of instruction and research.

In order to determine the times when additional personnel are needed to staff the reference desk, the author gathered and analyzed reference statistics for every hour of the week during the academic year 2001-2002. The following questions are attempted to be answered:

* Can heavy use days and times be identified?
* Is the same week each semester always the heaviest?
* Is there a significant variability in the number of questions during the semester?
* Can generalizable models be developed to help any library in scheduling for high and low use periods?

METHODOLOGY

This research study analyzes reference desk statistics collected daily and by the hour for the 2001-2002 academic year. These statistics are kept every year to satisfy the administrative requirements of HEGIS (Higher education information survey [Office of Education]) reports. The author used an Excel spreadsheet to enter the data by day and hours of the week for 53 weeks from August 2001 through July 2002. Table 1 shows the number of questions handled for the year by the hour. See the Appendix for statistical definitions.

The data in Table 1 are analyzed using standardized residuals from a chi-square test. The distribution of questions for all the 79 hours and 50 minutes that the library opened per week, and a professional librarian staffed the reference desk, are compared with a uniform (flat) distribution of the same number of questions. That is, if no difference in demand on staff at the reference desk existed as measured by the number of questions asked, then there would be no significant difference be-

TABLE 1. Number of Questions Per Hour of the Week

August 2001-July 2002

Time	Monday	Tuesday	Wednesday	Thursday	Friday	Saturday	Sunday
7:50-9 a.m.	101	103	97	130	99		
9-10	177	181	209	140	180		
10-11	204	238	271	208	212	107	
11-12	243	239	301	228	264	118	
12-1 p.m.	284	275	301	222	195	108	
1-2	252	242	296	213	191	99	
2-3	222	206	272	209	162	137	251
3-4	236	234	222	212	131	132	194
4-5	242	231	208	152	144		213
5-6	197	180	174	163			Break
6-7	193	203	124	113			134
7-8	191	218	152	120			101
8-9	172	163	115	90			70
9-10	158	148	101	85			76

tween the two distributions. Therefore, the author established a null hypothesis: no difference exists between the frequency distribution of a theoretically flat distribution of the same number of questions. The alternative hypothesis is that a difference does exist.

If a significant difference exists, then the standardized residuals need to be examined to determine the major contributors. If R (standardized residual) is greater than or equal to 2, the cell will be a major contributor to the significance (Dennison, p. 160). As the value of the cell grows larger, so does the contribution of the cell to the significance. Negative values are as significant as the positive values. The direction of the value simply shows if the major contributor deviates significantly above or below zero. The numeric value shows how great the deviation. The negative values indicate reduced staff needs as much as the positive values indicate increase in staffing needs.

ANALYSIS

The following results are obtained by using the method proposed above. Table 2 presents the residuals of the chi-square analysis.

TABLE 2. Chi-Square Residuals

	Monday	Tuesday	Wednesday	Thursday	Friday	Saturday	Sunday
7:50-9 a.m.	-6.04144	-5.81867	-6.41271	-3.81377	-6.11569		
9-10	-0.47227	-0.02673	2.052425	-3.07121	-0.10099		
10-11	1.45838	4.057326	6.507761	1.978169	2.275192	-5.52165	
11-12	4.280093	4.280093	8.735429	3.463281	6.136483	-4.70484	
12-1 p.m.	7.473084	6.953295	8.883941	3.017748	1.012846	-5.44739	
1-2	5.022649	7.992873	8.512663	2.349447	0.715824	-6.11569	
2-3	2.869237	1.829658	6.730528	2.052425	-1.43759	-3.29398	5.17116
3-4	3.983071	3.834559	2.943492	2.275192	-3.73951	-3.66526	0.938591
4-5	4.131582	3.686048	1.978169	-2.18014	-2.77419		2.497959
5-6	1.161358	-0.10099	-0.54652	-1.36333			
6-7	0.864335	1.606891	-4.2593	-5.07611			-3.66526
7-8	0.715824	2.720725	-2.18014	-4.55632			-5.96718
8-9	-0.69503	-1.36333	-4.9276	-6.78399			-8.2691
9-10	-1.73461	-2.47717	-5.96718	-7.15527			-13.467

173

This analysis showed variation in reference usage as is evident from the bolded numbers. Of the 79 hours and 50 minutes examined, 29 hours have a value of 2 or above and are thus positive contributors to the reference desk load. The negative numbers are as significant as the positive numbers, but they are not bolded because they are not yet being used to adjust staffing. Generally, the early morning hour of each day and late hours on Thursday through Saturday have significantly less reference usage. In general, significantly greater reference usage occurs on Monday from 11 a.m. to 5 p.m.; Tuesday from 10 a.m. to 1 p.m. and 3 p.m. to 5 p.m.; Wednesday from 9 a.m. to 4 p.m.; Thursday from 11 a.m. to 4 p.m.; Friday from 10 a.m. to 12 p.m.; and Sunday from 2 p.m. to 3 p.m. and 4 p.m. to 5 p.m., as indicated by the bold numbers.

As a result of this study, the Reference department at the Lupton Library implemented double staffing of the reference desk from 11 a.m. to 1 p.m. Monday through Thursday starting with the fall semester of September 2002. This decision was made on the bases of availability of the staff, instruction load, and convenience of scheduling, but not strictly according to these findings. During spring 2005, due to higher demand on instruction and also because two librarians left the department, librarians from other departments were pooled to fill in during 11 a.m. to 1 p.m. for the double staffing hours.

Since there is only one staff member on duty during weekends and nights, it cannot be further reduced without cutting some of the hours of service. Similarly, even though on Tuesdays from 7 p.m. to 8 p.m., Sundays from 2 p.m. to 3 p.m., and from 4 p.m. to 5 p.m., the load indicates a need for a second librarian. There is only one librarian on duty and this individual handles the problem of queuing, if it occurs. Most of the discussion in the literature, however, deals with the number of questions asked, the time lag between them, and the need to better utilize the professional librarian's time. This method identifies the high and low use times in this library. A well-trained paraprofessional could help during those times.

Graph 1 provides a visual representation of the data showing the load pattern during the week by time of day for the whole year.

The data is further sorted to determine the heaviest use weeks. Graph 2 displays the weekly number of questions received during the year 2001-2002. During the fall semester, the reference load is the heaviest starting with the third week of August till the end of November or the first week of December. For the spring semester, the reference load is heavy from January 21 through April 21.

GRAPH 1. Reference Questions by Time of Day

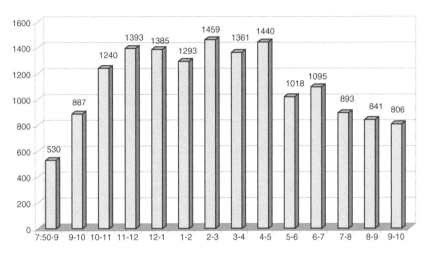

RANDOM SAMPLING METHOD

Starting with September 2002, the Lupton Library decided to collect reference statistics by a random sampling method. By using the actual data for 2001-2002 for the number of patrons assisted at the reference desk, a standard of deviation is calculated for the entire year and also for each semester (Table 3). A confidence level of 95% and an acceptable error of ± 5 patrons are chosen. The following formula is used:

$$n = (z \, (s)/e)^2$$

Where n = sample size needed, z = the accuracy estimate (for 95% confidence this is equal to 1.96 standard deviation units), s = standard of deviation (Table 3) and e = acceptable error (100-95 = 5). As an example, the calculation of the sample size needed for medium-usage period, estimated to the nearest whole number for the year 2001-2002, is illustrated below:

$$n = ((1.96 \, (29.56)/5)^2 = 136 \text{ days}$$

Table 4 gives the standard of deviations for the year, as well as for the fall, spring, and summer semesters of 2001-2002. Based on that were calculated the number of days to be sampled during 2002-2003 (Table 5).

GRAPH 2. Weekly Number of Reference Questions

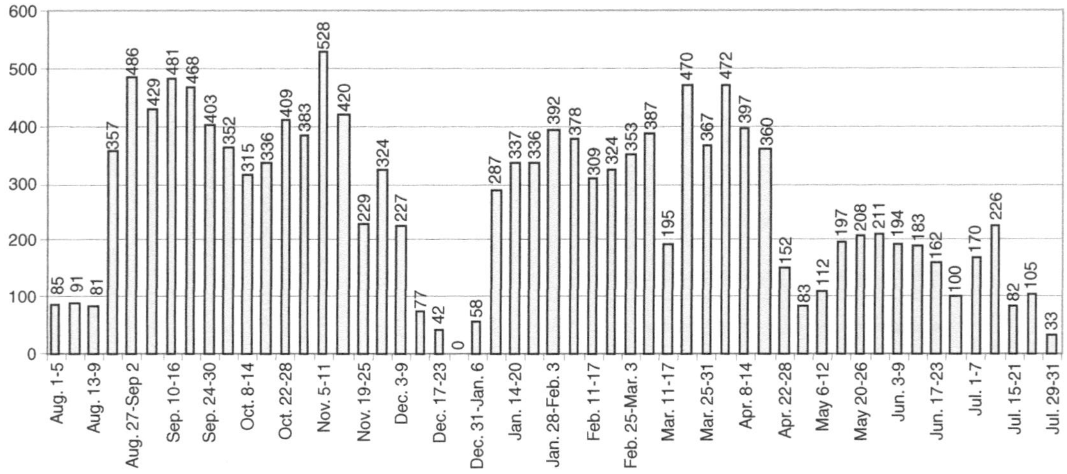

TABLE 3. Analysis of the Number of Reference Enquiries Received During 2001-2002

Column1	Yearly 2001-2002	Fall 2001-2002	Spring 2001-2002	Summer 2001-2002
Mean	38.14	41.73	47.01	21.86
Standard Error	1.55	2.95	2.60	1.56
Median	33	35.5	44	22
Mode	0	0	0	0
Standard Deviation*	29.56	33.16	28.39	14.87
Sample Variance	873.73	1099.76	806.036	221.28
Kurtosis	−0.34	−0.89	−0.68	−0.74
Skewness	0.68	0.43	0.28	0.25
Range	125	120	122	58
Minimum	0	0	0	0
Maximum	125	120	122	58
Sum	13884	5258	5595	1989
Count	364	126	119	91
Confidence Level (95.0%)	3.05	5.85	5.15	3.09

*Standard of deviation is based on daily count.

Required Sample Size for the Number of Days/Random Sampling of Patrons Reference Department/UTC Lupton Library 2002-2003

95% confidence level

$\sigma = .05 \quad Error = \pm 5 \, patrons$

$$n = \frac{(19.96 * 29.55)^2}{5} * 136 \, days \, of \, sampling$$

n = total sample size, σ = the standard of deviation, n_i = the stratum sample size for the i^t stratum
Ni = the size of the ith stratum, σ_j = the standard of deviation for the ith stratum

TABLE 4. Number of Days for Collecting Statistics During Each Semester, 2002-2003

Term	Ni	σi	Ni * σi	# of Sampling days 2002-2003
Fall	126	33.16	4178.16	(91*33.16)/8909.74*136 = 64 days
Summer	91	14.87	1353.17	(98*14.87)/8909.74*136 = 21 days
Spring	119	28.39	3378.41	(119*28.39)/8909.74*136 = 52 days
Sum of Semesters			8909.74	

Table 4 shows the number of calculated sampling days (within a 95% confidence interval).

TABLE 5. Monthly Count of Reference Questions for Actual 2001-2002, Sampled Counts 2002-2003 and 2003-2004

Months	Actual Count 2001-2002	Sample Count 2002-2003	Sample Count 2003-2004
July	616	608	682
Aug	1100	917	1622
Sep	1781	2178	2502
Oct	1805	1640	1892
Nov	1501	1793	1725
Dec	404	526	763
Jan	1352	1689	1414
Feb	1364	1375	1351
Mar	1419	1637	1414
Apr	1464	1369	1096
May	728	524	632
June	645	623	600
Total	14179	14879	15754

Table 4 gives the standard of deviations for the year, as well as for the fall, spring, and summer semesters of 2001-2002. Based on that were calculated the number of days to be sampled during 2002-2003 (Table 5).

Once the number of days of sampling needed for each period is determined, a randomized sampling schedule is developed using a random number table. All days on which the library is open throughout the year are numbered consecutively. The numbers in the random scheduling tables are prepared for this program, then, indicated the days throughout the year for which the statistics are to be kept. For fall 2002, 64 sampling days were determined out of the 126 days the library was open; for the summer 2003, 21 sampling days are determined out of the 91 days the library was open; and for the spring 2003, 52 sampling days are determined out of the 119 days the library was open. On the days identified as sample days, data is collected during all open hours.

By keeping statistics on the calculated number of days above, the sampler can be 95% sure that the number of patrons the sample indicated for the year is within plus/minus 5 patrons of what the actual number of patrons would have been if data was collected every day.

The average number of patrons (i.e., the mean) assisted per day is 38 (Table 3). The range of questions asked was from 0 to 125 (Graph 2). The weekly count ranged from 0 to 528. The only week recording zero statistics is the week of December 24-30 when the library closed.

Throughout the year, many time periods occurred when no reference statistics are recorded. This is due to the librarian being too busy to record numbers, just simply forgetting to record, or there are no questions asked. But they do not fall into any pattern.

Table 5 gives the monthly count of the number of questions answered at the reference desk during the 2001-2002 and the sample years 2002-2003 and 2003-2004. On the whole, the number of the reference questions handled during the year 2002-2003 show an increase of 2.8% and 2003-2004 by 11% (sampling years) than the number of reference questions handled in 2001-2002 (actual daily count). But when analyzed by using the standard error of means formula (Standard error of means = $\sigma / \sqrt{n}$), at 95% confidence level, the difference between the actual and the sample means and their standard error for the years 2001-2002 and 2003-2004 is within the acceptable range. Since the numbers for 2002-2003 are even lower than 2003-2004, it is concluded that the sample statistics can serve the accountability requirements. Graph 3 gives a comparison of the data by months for the year 2001-2002 with the sampled years of 2002-2003 and 2003-2004. As the numbers indicate, the spring and the fall semesters are busier than the summer semester for each of those years. Starting with the third week of

GRAPH 3. Monthly Count of Reference Questions 2001-2004

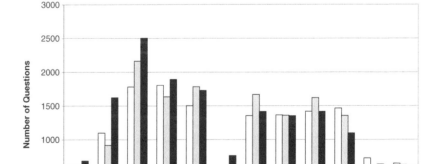

□ Actual Count 2001-2002   ▨ Sample Count 2002-2003   ■ Sample Count 2003-2004

August till the end of November or first week of December, the load is heavy during the fall semester. During the spring semester from January through April, the load is heavy. May, June, July, and December are lighter months.

The next step is to determine if the data collected by the random sampling method for the years 2002-2003 and 2003-2004 also show some similar characteristics as 2001-2002. The number of questions for the day of the week for sample days for 2002-2003 and 2003-2004 are entered into Excel spreadsheets and compared with the same day of the week with the year 2001-2002. For example, all Mondays for which the data is collected are compared with the Monday of the same week in 2002-2003 and 2003-2004 (if sampled). The following few graphs show a somewhat similar trend in the number of questions handled at the reference desk (see Graphs 4-7).

CATEGORIES OF QUESTIONS

Starting with September 2002, the reference questions are divided into two categories: internal (coming from patrons in the library) and external (coming from patrons outside the library by phone). Each of these two categories is further divided into three subdivisions: (1) directional questions, (2) less than five minutes questions, and (3) more than five minute questions. Standard definitions are also added to the three types of questions. Tables 6 and 7 show the pattern of the distribution of those questions. Graph 8 and Graph 9 show the percentage of questions in each of those categories.

The statistics for the above two years show that the greatest numbers (66% to 70%) of reference questions come from internal users and take less than five minutes to answer. The directional questions range from 8% to 11% for internal users and 2% to 3% from external users. All those questions that take more than five minutes, however, involve variables such as orienting the student to the library catalog, the databases or database links to which library subscribes, and other print or online sources. It involves teaching the patron as to how to use the same sources efficiently. For some users who are not computer savvy, it may even take longer and may take one or two such repeated sessions. This is remindful of a remark made by one of the librarians on the statistics sheet, "It took forever to answer that one question." The main goal is to get more help with answering questions at the reference desk so that the

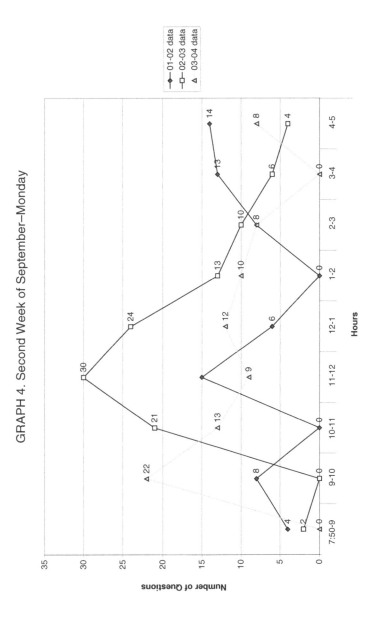

GRAPH 4. Second Week of September–Monday

01-02 data
02-03 data
03-04 data

Number of Questions

Hours

181

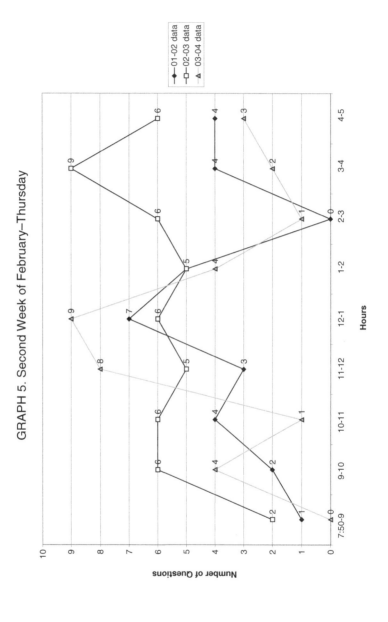

GRAPH 5. Second Week of February–Thursday

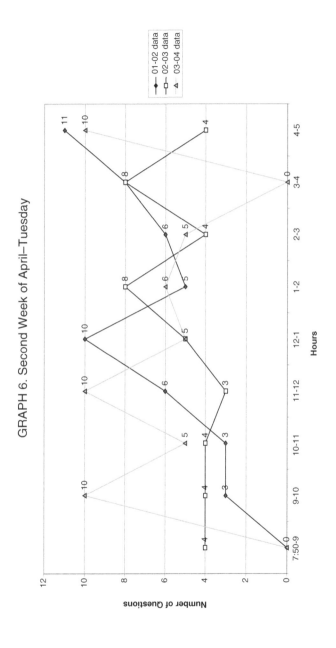

GRAPH 6. Second Week of April–Tuesday

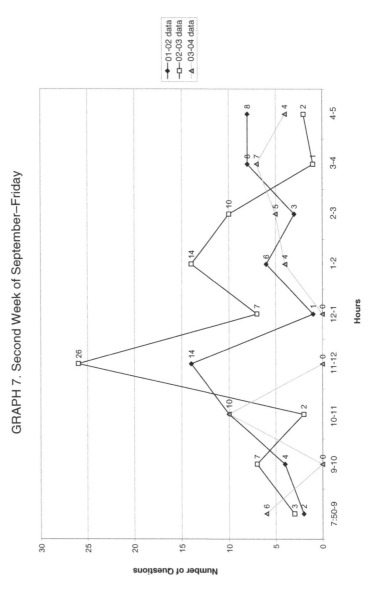

GRAPH 7. Second Week of September–Friday

Legend:
◆ 01-02 data
□ 02-03 data
▲ 03-04 data

Number of Questions (y-axis): 0, 5, 10, 15, 20, 25, 30

Hours (x-axis): 7:50-9, 9-10, 10-11, 11-12, 12-1, 1-2, 2-3, 3-4, 4-5

TABLE 6. Reference Desk Statistics 2002-2003

	Internal Users			External Users				
	Directional	Less than 5 minutes	More than 5 minutes	Directional	Less than 5 minutes	More than 5 minutes	E-mail Questions	Monthly Totals
Month								
July							4	
August							13	
September	211	1555	197	38	143	20	14	2178
October	137	1183	141	30	121	21	7	1640
November	139	1373	143	14	113	0	11	1793
December	5	410	30	30	40	0	11	526
January	127	1205	80	22	213	19	23	1689
February	104	927	137	18	168	4	17	1375
March	79	1158	124	23	232	4	17	1637
April	98	1019	98	14	112	14	14	1369
May	68	325	29	21	66	7	8	524
June	54	377	54	25	104	7	2	623
Yearly Totals	1022	9532	1033	235	1312	96	141	13354

Note: The breakdown of reference questions into internal and external users and the subdivisions of data into directional, < than 5 minutes and > than 5 minutes started in September of 2002.

librarians do not feel rushed in performing their duty. Some of these reference questions a professional librarian carries home long after the patron leaves the library; as Dr. S. R. Ranganathan (1961) stated, "A reference librarian sleeps and eats with reference questions" (p. v.).

CONCLUSION

Even though reference service is essentially a human science, efforts are underway to automate and standardize as many aspects of this service as possible. In order to improve the efficiency and productivity of the reference service, it is essential to measure various aspects of the entire reference process. Literature research shows that, since the 1980s, the major university libraries are collecting reference use data and analyzing it by standard statistical methods. This is done to see if some standards can be developed which could be applied across the board.

TABLE 7. Reference Desk Statistics 2003-2004

	Internal Users			External Users				
	Directional	Less than 5 minutes	More than 5 minutes	Directional	Less than 5 minutes	More than 5 minutes	E-mail Questions	Monthly Totals
Month								
July	48	411	67	25	115	12	4	682
August	232	1126	80	31	116	17	20	1622
September	248	1844	150	32	184	24	20	2502
October	181	1354	153	31	134	16	24	1893
November	143	1260	113	45	145	10	9	1725
December	121	440	44	50	94	5	9	763
January	209	960	116	33	102	14	10	1444
February	172	872	157	37	83	11	19	1351
March	65	976	211	21	140	10	21	1444
April	100	665	177	28	83	27	16	1096
May	62	363	79	31	76	7	14	632
June	82	312	88	30	76	8	4	600
Yearly Totals	1663	10583	1435	394	1348	161	170	15754

The data taken as the base for the statistical analysis for this study are the number of questions asked at the reference desk for the year 2001-2002, when the statistics are kept for every hour of the week the reference desk is open and a reference librarian is on duty. The methods used chi-square residuals and descriptive statistical analysis.

During 2002-2004, the reference use statistics are gathered by a random sampling method. When data is compared from week to week for the random sample years with the year 2001-2002 when the data is collected by every hour for every day of the week, an almost similar pattern is revealed. Heavy days, weeks, hours, and months fell into a similar pattern from semester to semester and from year to year. Significant variability is evidenced from depth analysis of the data in the number of questions posed at the reference desk from hour to hour and from day to day and also from semester to semester in this academic library.

With the ease of availability of web-based reference service it seems, and as is evidenced by the data above, the number of questions at or off

GRAPH 8. Percentage of Reference Questions 2003-2004

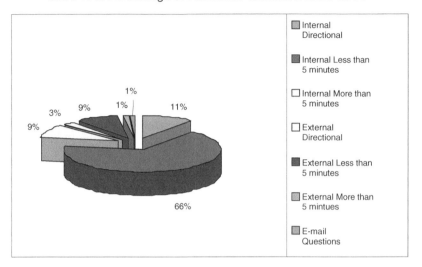

GRAPH 9. Percentage of Reference Questions 2002-2003

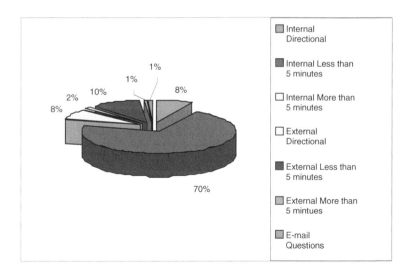

of the reference desk is likely to go up. Coffman and Saxton (1999) and Rettig (2004) also visualize that networked libraries will be serving greater number of patrons and for longer hours. The types of questions posed at the reference desk are also getting more complex, and finding the right information and/or complete information is more time consuming. Raising the level of computer skills of each patron to enable him/her to use online sources efficiently takes time. Richardson (2002) is correct in stating, "The probability of an individual finding valuable and complete information is not only dependent on the librarian's reference skills, but is also predicted by the user's familiarity with the library and his/her level of education" (p. 42).

Holistic computing is allowing libraries to incorporate tools and software needed for data analysis with the information and data needing manipulation, and all from a single interface (Coffman & Saxton, p. 142). This study suggests that statistical analyses of reference transaction counts can be used as a method for documenting how busy a library is at a particular time. Managers can make sound decisions about the staffing needs at the reference desk based on such studies. Now that the economics of library services and the nature of information as a commodity is being analyzed in depth, the profession is experiencing visibility, maturity, growth, and appreciation.

REFERENCES

Blandy, S. G., Martin, L. M., and Strife, M. L., eds. (1992). *Assessment and accountability in reference work.* Binghamton, N.Y.: The Haworth Press, Inc.

Bundt, J. (2000). Strategic stewards: Managing accountability, building trust. *Journal of Public Administration Research & Theory, 10*(4), 757-778.

Chu, F. (1997). Another look at staffing the reference desk. *College & Research Library News, 58*(10), 713.

Coffman, S., and Saxton, M. (1999). Staffing the reference desk in the largely-digital library. *The Reference Librarian,* 66, 141-63.

Cummins, T. R. (1992). Developing personnel and staffing standards. *Library Administration & Management,* 6(4):182-186.

Dennison, R. F. (1999). Usage-based staffing of the reference desk: A statistical approach. *Reference & User Services Quarterly, 39*(2), 158-65.

Glockner, B. (2004). Accountability and accreditation for special libraries: It can be done! *The Australian Library Journal,* 53(3), 277-284.

Kantor, P. B. (1984). *Objective performance measures for academic and research libraries.* Washington, D.C. Association of Research Libraries.

Kesselman, M., & Watstein, S. B. (1987). The measurement of reference and information services. *The Journal of Academic Librarianship, 13*(1), 24-30.

Kuhlman, J. R. (1995). On the economics of reference service: Toward a heuristic model for an uncertain world. *The Reference Librarian*, 49/50, 25-43.

Lochstet, G., & Lehman, D. H. (1999). A correlation method for collecting reference statistics. *College and Research Libraries*, 60(1), 45-53.

Maxstadt, J. M. (1988). A new approach to reference statistics. *College & Research Libraries News*, 49(2), 85-86, 88.

Murgai, S. R. (1986). Future challenges in library science. *The Georgia Librarian*, 23(3), 68-69.

Ranganathan, S. R. (1961). *Reference service*. London: Asia Publishing House.

Rettig, J. (2004). *Interview on the future of the academic library*. Retrieved July 20, 2005, from http://faculty.jscc.edu/scohen/rettiginterview.html.

Richardson, J. V., Jr. (2002). Reference is better than we thought. *Library Journal*, 127(7), 41-42.

Schlesinger, A. (1997). *Staffing pattern questions at the Cleveland Heights-University Heights public library*. (Report No. IR 057 232). Cleveland, OH: A Master's Research Paper submitted to the Kent State University School of Library Science. (ERIC Document Reproduction Service No. ED424867).

Summerhill, K. S. (1994). The high cost of reference: The need to reassess services and service delivery. *The Reference Librarian*, 43, 71-85.

Taylor, A. (1994). Plan for service: Professional and non-professional reference staff. *The Reference Librarian*, 43, 101-105.

Witucke, V., & Schumaker, C. J. (1991). Analyzing reference activities: The affordable solution. *RQ*, 31(1), 58-69.

APPENDIX. Definitions of Statistical Terms

Chi-Square test: is a test for "goodness of the fit" between observed values (O) as computed and expected values (E) (Flat or uniform values, usually the mean). A statistical test calculated as a sum of squares of observed values minus the expected values divided by the expected values. $(O-E)^2/E$

Uniform Distribution: The probability distribution if a random variable having constant probability over an interval.

Standard error: The standard of deviation of the errors of sampling distribution of a statistic.

R = Residual: The difference between the actual value of a single measurement minus the computed value regarded as the most probable value is often the arithmetic mean of a number of similar measurements, the residual then being a deviation from the mean. It is also called residual error and error of estimate. The residuals are ordinarily squared.

Null Hypotheses: The "no difference" or "association" hypotheses to be tested against an alternative hypothesis.

SOURCES

Everitt, B. S. (2002). *The Cambridge Dictionary of Statistics*. 2nd edition. Cambridge: Cambridge University Press.

Kurtz, A. K., & Edgerton, Harold A. (1967). Statistical Dictionary of Terms and Symbols. New York: Hafner Publishing.

Index

Page numbers followed by f indicate figures; those marked with t indicate tables; those marked with g indicate graphs.

For Product Safety Concerns and Information please contact
our EU representative GPSR@taylorandfrancis.com Taylor & Francis
Verlag GmbH, Kaufingerstraße 24, 80331 München, Germany

T - #0124 - 270225 - C1 - 212/152/12 - PB - 9780789031945 - Gloss Lamination